What is Philosophy of Religion?

Polity's *What is Philosophy?* series

Sparkling introductions to the key topics in philosophy, written with zero jargon by leading philosophers.

What is Philosophy of Religion?

Charles Taliaferro

polity

First published in 2019 by Polity Press

Polity Press
65 Bridge Street
Cambridge CB2 1UR, UK

Polity Press
101 Station Landing
Suite 300
Medford, MA 02155, USA

ISBN-13: 978-1-5095-2954-4
ISBN-13: 978-1-5095-2955-1(pb)

A catalogue record for this book is available from the British Library.

Typeset in 11 on 13 pt Sabon by Toppan Best-set Premedia Limited
Printed and bound in Great Britain by CPI Group (UK) Ltd, Croydon

The publisher has used its best endeavours to ensure that the URLs for external websites referred to in this book are correct and active at the time of going to press. However, the publisher has no responsibility for the websites and can make no guarantee that a site will remain live or that the content is or will remain appropriate.

Every effort has been made to trace all copyright holders, but if any have been overlooked the publisher will be pleased to include any necessary credits in any subsequent reprint or edition.

For further information on Polity, visit our website: politybooks.com

Contents

Acknowledgments

I thank Pascal Porcheron for inviting me to write *What is Philosophy of Religion?* I am also very grateful for the excellent assistance of Ellen MacDonald-Kramer. I thank Glenn Gordon, "Saint" Andrew Lupton, and Emma Claire dePaulo Reid for epic help in editing and revising the manuscript. I also thank Fiona Ellis and an anonymous reviewer for their insightful, incisive recommendations.

I thank Itayli Marquette, Wael Awada, and especially Tim Crane for the final preparation of the manuscript.

This book is dedicated to the many students I have had the joy of working with in the course Philosophical Theology at St. Olaf College over twenty years (and continuing). Most recently these include Anders, Andrew, Benj, Carly ("Cheryl"), Elliot, Erica, Hannah Joy, Michael, Katherine, Jess, Bay, Diane, Rose, and Wael. This book is also dedicated, with great admiration, to the exemplary professor of philosophy of religion Mikael Stenmark of Uppsala University, Sweden, who recognizes and promotes the international, collaborative practice of philosophy of religion. He is especially admirable in his sensitivity in placing the critical engagement of religious and secular traditions in the context of authentic care for, and respect of, persons and positions. Without such evident respect, even well thought out, responsible analysis may well come across as callous, uninformed cultural confrontation.

This manuscript was completed in the company of the inspiring Jil Evans (American artist and writer extraordinaire), the Polichs of Dover Street, and Elizabeth and Ryan, true lovers of wisdom.

Introduction

Is there a God? If there is, what is the relationship between God and the cosmos? Can we experience or perceive God? Does it matter whether some religious vision of the divine or sacred is true or false? When it comes to religion, should we be less concerned with truth and falsehood, and more with matters of personal fulfillment and satisfaction? How important is it for religious faith to be based upon evidence? If it is important, what kind of evidence should it be based upon? Has contemporary science shown religious beliefs to be superstitious and false? Are our concepts of good and evil rooted in religious concepts of life? If there is an all-powerful, all-good God, why is there so much evil in the world? Is there a soul? When, if ever, might it be reasonable or wise to believe in divine revelation, miracles, an incarnation of the divine or life after death? Are different religions different paths to the same sacred reality? How should we evaluate disagreements over religious beliefs? For example, should your confidence in your beliefs about God be reduced because others, who seem equally as intelligent and sincere as you, do not share those beliefs?

These are only some of the questions that animate philosophy of religion. They involve virtually every area of philosophy, impacting our political and personal values, our perspective on reality, the nature and limits of what we can know about or hope for, and so on. Today, philosophy of religion is undertaken by philosophers coming from all the great religious and secular perspectives: some are deeply skeptical about the truth of religions; others are observant Jews, practicing Christians, Muslims, Hindus, Buddhists, Daoists, and practitioners of other religious traditions. There are even philosophers who propose new models and concepts of God that go beyond and challenge historical and contemporary religions.

Philosophical reflection on matters of religious significance is the oldest form of philosophy in both East and West. In Ancient Greece, Socrates and the Pre-Socratics (those philosophers who flourished prior to Socrates) were very much concerned with the nature of the divine and the authority of the will of God and/or the gods. In China, philosophers who practiced Confucianism and Daoism pondered *tian* (heaven) deeply. While *tian* and the Dao (the Way) are not the same as the concept of the divine in Ancient Greece—or in Judaism, Christianity, and Islam—they are conceived of as a way of life involving reverential awe, which many see as spiritual or central to religious life. Similarly, in ancient Indian philosophy we find deep spiritually engaging reflections on Brahman, the self, avatars (manifestations of the divine in this life), the Buddha's teaching on suffering and enlightenment, Nirvana, and more. The practice of philosophy of religion today shows itself to have value, in part, because of its long lineage in terms of the whole history of thought and culture.

Philosophical reflection on religion is also of immense contemporary significance due to the modern and historical role of religions in shaping societies and personal lives. Philosophy of religion engages with living practices and beliefs held by millions of people, rather than focusing on abstract topics that do not affect the lives of people today. One reason why many introduction to philosophy textbooks over the past fifty years have begun with philosophy of religion is to show readers how the study of philosophy can lead us to critically engage with pervasive human practices.

Philosophy of religion is also important in that it takes seriously deep questions about the meaning of our lives. Arguably, if one of the main teachings of Buddhism is true, then our pursuit of power, wealth, and pleasure, and our belief in a continuous individual ego—that we are each substantial selves enduring over time—are actually in some sense an illusion. According to this view, a life of greedy self-aggrandizement turns out to be a life in the service of that which is not fundamentally real. What we think of as a fulfilling life is actually just our ongoing contribution to the wheel of rebirth (samsāra). Taking up another alternative, if there is no God, then those of us who think we are praying to God are not actually praying to someone who hears us and responds; we are instead addressing an image or projection of something not real. On the other hand, if there actually is an omnipresent, unsurpassably good God, then those of us who ignore or deny the existence of this God may be missing a vital, life-enhancing relationship with communities of believers who live in the light of this sacred, awesome, transcendent reality. Although I will not argue for the point here, I would suggest that an exploration of the meaning of life should be at the heart of higher education—and not only at the university or college level, but also as part of the broader task of lifelong learning. How much meaning should we give to, or recognize in, our personal relationships, our goals, what we love, like and hate? If it seems to you that such questions are central to the meaning of your life, then you have a reason to pursue philosophy of religion.

In one sense of the word, this book is an exercise in what may be called *apologetics*. Apologetics is a technical term for making a case for a given position. The apologetic aim of this book is to make a case *not* for the truth of any particular religion or any secular, non-religious alternative, *but for the value of philosophy of religion itself*. In the final chapter, I suggest ways in which you might participate in contemporary philosophy of religion, whether you believe there is a God, are atheistic or agnostic, Hindu or Buddhist, or a follower of Judaism, Christianity, Islam or any other religious path. Regardless of your position, which itself may change over time, you need not look upon philosophy of religion as a spectator, but can engage with it as a participant. While other introductory philosophical books include guidelines for further study in an appendix or epilogue, I have put such material (and more) in the main text in order to encourage *each* reader to participate in the field of philosophy of religion.

I was drawn to philosophy of religion for at least three reasons, which may attract you to the subject as well. First, I did not want simply to accept uncritically the religious tradition I was brought up in. Philosophy of religion is a domain in which to investigate the religion of your birth, or your secular upbringing, and other religions and secular alternatives. Questioning one's own religion can be a way, not necessarily to give up the faith of one's upbringing, but to make a particular religion one's own, to discover reasons why one might practice it rather than simply accepting an inheritance from family and culture (as important as such an inheritance is). I have personally found that doubt and questioning can be positive factors in the growth of religious faith, both for myself and for my students. My hope is that you too will find philosophy of religion to be an exciting, healthy exploration of alternative views of the world and spiritual practices.

Second, my generation (late "baby boomers") grew up in the midst of fierce disagreements, both cultural and personal, and found enormous relief in the domain of philosophy of religion (and philosophy in general), where there is a commitment to calm, fair-minded and non-manipulative dialogue. We came of age in the United States during the Vietnam War, the Cold War, the Civil Rights movement, and the assassinations of President John F. Kennedy, his brother Bobby, Martin Luther King, Jr., and Malcolm X. Today, there seem to be just as many disputes over the nature of a democratic republic, terrorism, racism and sexism, nuclear proliferation, climate change, and more. I was driven then (and now) to explore how religious traditions might be part of the problem, or might provide a solution to social ills. In the practice of philosophy in general, and of philosophy of religion in particular, I discovered philosophers respectfully listening to each other, weighing arguments and reasoning, with the aim of practicing the love of wisdom: the literal meaning of the term "philosophy," derived from the Greek *philein* (meaning *to love*) and *sophia* (meaning *wisdom*). In philosophy, arguments are (ideally) not motivated by vanity, jealousy, envy, rage, hatred, or intimidation. While it is wise to recognize that none of us is perfect, and so the complete eradication of some kind of self-interest may not be possible, the goal of loving wisdom (again, ideally) should be an open-minded, respectful exchange of ideas, rather than self-seeking competition. Philosophical arguments are very unlike what we would commonly label in English as *quarrels*. Quarrels frequently involve unfriendly, even hostile disputes, whereas among philosophers arguments often occur between those who share a bond of friendship and a mutual desire for clarity, coherence, and the refining of each other's line of reasoning. You, too, might find philosophy of religion a source of energizing respect, and a refuge from today's divisive quarreling.

Third, I was drawn into philosophy of religion because of its capacity to connect people from different cultures around the world. As a young person, I studied Christianity in North America and Europe, Judaism in Israel, Islam in Turkey, Iran, Pakistan, and Afghanistan, Hinduism and Buddhism in India and Nepal. This was not, initially, a matter of deep scholarship, but nor was it conventional tourism: not only because I was held up at gunpoint in Afghanistan, where I spent a few hours in jail, but also because I earned college credits for reading (in translation) sacred texts, attending lectures (including one by the guru sage Jiddu Krishnamurti in India), visiting holy sites, and writing philosophical essays that were ferociously critiqued by my skeptical college philosophy professor back in Vermont. Later, as a graduate student, and now as a professor of philosophy of religion, I have continued to seek to make connections between people, offering a course in philosophy of religion in China, meeting with students and professors in Europe, Iran, South America, Russia, Canada, and elsewhere. Some of my research projects have involved collaboration with over 400 philosophers of religion from around the world (as was the case with the forthcoming five-volume work, *The Wiley-Blackwell Encyclopedia of Philosophy of Religion*).

The United Nations has declared that on the third Thursday in November, every year, people around the world should be encouraged to practice philosophy. I have used those Thursdays to connect my students at St. Olaf College with students globally. For two years, I arranged for my students in North America to converse philosophically with students in Iran, via the internet and an exchange of videos. As I write this introduction, the governments of the United States and the Islamic Republic of Iran are not on friendly terms, but that does not mean that the students in our countries cannot explore common bonds, in this case through philosophy of religion. The importance of philosophy in assisting people's shared search for insight and peace, and for the avoidance of prejudice, is captured in this statement from former UNESCO Director-General Irina Bokova:

> Faced with the complexity of today's world, philosophical reflection is above all a call to humility, to take a step back and engage in reasoned dialogue, to build together the solutions to challenges that are beyond our control. This is the best way to educate enlightened citizens, equipped to fight stupidity and prejudice. The greater the difficulties encountered the greater the need for philosophy to make sense of questions of peace and sustainable development. (UNESCO 2017)

I add that the experience of connecting my students with those of a Muslim philosophy professor in Tehran was not just educational (we reflected together on the eleventh-century *A Treatise of Love* by the brilliant Muslim philosopher Ibn Sina), it was fun. (I am very attracted to the great seventeenth-century French essayist Montaigne's idea that effective education can be both serious and entertaining at the same time.)

I end this introduction with a few more observations on the practice of philosophy and the definition of the term "religion."

The practice of philosophy: In practicing philosophy of religion it is a good idea to adopt what might be called the *Philosophical Golden Rule*. That is, that it is good to treat the philosophy of others as you would like your own to be treated. This can enhance the respect and openness of philosophical exchanges, which might otherwise be defensive or insensitive to the merits of other points of view. I would also commend *Philosophical Good Samaritan Practices*. The idea of being a Good Samaritan (the phrase is taken from a parable in the New Testament) is that of helping out persons in need. In this context then, when your peers are in philosophical trouble (when, for example, your dialogue partner

has failed to see how her position might be more effectively presented), it is a virtue to come to their aid, if
you are able to do so, even if you disagree with them.
In this regard, philosophical debate is very different
from adversarial debate in law courts. Overall, I would
suggest that, ideally, philosophy is fundamentally non-
strategic in the traditional and common use of the term
"strategy" (derived from the Greek *strategia*, meaning
"the office or command of a general"), as practiced in
the military, in business, and in sports in which decep-
tion may be called for (where players, like generals and
business competitors, frequently attempt to conceal
their intentions). Instead, when advancing some argument or philosophical theory, it is a mark of proper
humility and the love of wisdom to freely admit when
one is uncertain or has doubts about some of the claims
or arguments one is advancing.

This spirit of the love of wisdom was dramatically
revealed to me in graduate school. At a huge meeting
of the American Philosophical Association (the largest
philosophical society in the United States), my philosophy professor and mentor's views were criticized by
another philosopher. After hearing the objections, my
professor rose to the podium and simply said that his
critic's objections were excellent and that his thesis was
mistaken. His example stood out for me then, and still
does so today, as an ideal way to practice the love of
wisdom, rather than clinging to our ideas because they
are our ideas and, understandably, it is only natural for
us to want to be right.

Another important element to stress in the practice
of philosophy of religion is sympathetic imagination. A
few philosophers have argued that religious traditions
cannot really be adequately addressed by "outsiders."
By their lights, you have to be a believer or a practitioner of a religious tradition in order even to understand it. In his book *Divine Faith*, John Lamont makes
this claim:

> This perspective—of the believer—cannot be the same
> as that of an unbeliever ... An unbeliever cannot properly
> evaluate the reasonableness of Christian faith, because
> the evidence necessary for such an evaluation is not
> available to him. The only way for him to find out
> whether faith is reasonable is to, as far as lies in him,
> take the venture of believing. (Lamont 2004: 216)

Perhaps there are some domains of inquiry in which
Lamont is right. It may be difficult to engage in a philosophy of romantic love, for example, if one has not
had even an inkling of the experience of such love
oneself. Quite possibly, if you wish to contribute to a
philosophy of romantic love, it would be desirable, as
far as it lies within you, to try to fall in love. Likewise,
it might be easier for someone who is or has been a
Hindu to understand Hinduism. But in terms of exploring religion, I suggest that Lamont is underestimating
the scope and power of imagination (and this might
also be true of romantic love). I know of no compelling reason to doubt that a non-Christian can form an
adequate idea of what it would be like to experience
the world through the lens of Christian faith and practice. Arguably, there are abundant cases, historically
and today, where Christian and non-Christian philosophers have engaged in fruitful, shared philosophical
inquiry into the justifications for and objections against
Christian faith. There are even cases when an "out-
sider" can understand a religious faith even better than
the "insiders," as when the atheist French existential-
ist philosopher, Albert Camus, spoke about the need
for Christians to stand up against torture and injustice
in a talk he gave at a Dominican monastery in 1948
(later published as "The Unbeliever and Christians").
Lamont's position would also lend support to a paradoxical view of religious conversion, for if he is right it
would seem that no one would have access to the evidence of the truth of a religion until or unless one had

converted to it, whereas at least some people appear to embrace a religion on the basis of what they think are evident reasons.

Defining the term "religion". One reason why it is desirable to have a stable understanding of what counts as a religion is because in some countries there are laws governing religion. For example, in the United States there is a Constitutional precept that there should be a separation between church and state (where the term "church" is now more broadly interpreted to include non-Christian religions). It will not work to define religion as, say, *a practice in which people worship God*, because among what today most of us recognize as religions there are those that do not involve a God. Most forms of Buddhism do not include God; and Daoism and Confucianism do not include the worship of God. A more promising way to define religion would be by giving examples: *Religions include Judaism, Christianity, Islam, Hinduism, and Buddhism and traditions like them.* Definitions by example can be respectful. Definitions of visual colors in a dictionary sometimes involve reproducing the colors red, orange, yellow, and so on. Alternatives, such as defining colors in terms of waves of light (between 4,000 and 7,000 Angstrom units), would not give the reader a handle on how to recognize the visual experience of color, but only an understanding of the causes of our seeing colors, which would include not just wavelengths, but retinas, the visual cortex, and so on. But while giving examples in the case of visual colors may be adequate (at least for non-color blind observers), in the definition of "religion" it is desirable for us to be explicit about what it is that makes Judaism, Hinduism, Buddhism, and so on, religions. It is partly desirable in order to avoid falling into a conventionalism that simply accepts the status quo and potentially excludes traditions or communities that should be recognized (for better or worse) as religions, even if they do not strongly resemble our standard set of recognized religions. (There might be a similar handicap in defining colors by example, insofar as it tempts us to believe that the only color sensations are those experienced by humans.)

Here is an alternative definition of religion that aims at offering more guidance than can be gained simply by giving examples:

A religion involves a communal, transmittable body of teachings and prescribed practices about an ultimate, sacred reality or state of being that calls for reverence or awe, a body which guides its practitioners into what it describes as a saving, illuminating or emancipatory relationship to this reality through a personally transformative life of prayer, ritualized meditation, and/or moral practices like repentance and personal regeneration.

The above definition stresses that religions are not only (or exclusively) matters of cognition but also involve affective change; in a phrase: *religions do not seek only to inform but to transform.*

I am sure that more than one reader will be able to point out some mistake in, or suggest an important improvement to, this proposed definition (a variation of which appears in *A Dictionary of Philosophy of Religion*, second edition, which I co-edited with Elsa Marty), and, following the practice of my mentor professor, I hope that I will have the humility to admit the error and revise the definition accordingly. But, for now, I suggest that it is sufficiently broad so as not to define religion in terms that are exclusive of some religions and not others. For example, the definition does not entail that *all religions* include some element that is specific only to one or to several (but not all) world religions. I believe it would be a mistake, for instance, to propose that all religions include a condemnation of "sin." Sin involves violating the will and nature of a Creator-God, but because not all religions acknowledge such a God, the concept is too restrictive to function as a defining quality of a religion. In Buddhism, for example, rather than sin, there is stress on the ills that result from wrong action, wrong attachment (craving), and illusion.

From time to time in this book you are invited to attend to definitions of concepts and the clarification of terms. In both the West and East, historically and today, most philosophers have paid attention to the clarity and meaning of the terms we use, in order to better enable us to mean what we say, and to say what we mean. In Confucianism, for example, it is held that clarifying and refining speech ("the rectification of names") is essential for social harmony. This drive for clarity and refinement was also very much an element of Socrates' practice of philosophy. In the earliest portraits we have of Socrates, he challenges us to be clear about our language, lest we commit an injustice.

Here is an overview of what lies ahead. Chapter 1 considers the relationship between religion and science. Chapter 2 examines some of the teachings and practices of world religions and how they might impact what may be called the meaning of life. Chapter 3 ponders some of the major philosophical work on the concept of God. Chapter 4 considers some of the evidence for and against the world religions. Chapter 5 tackles the problem of evil and religious teachings about goodness. Chapter 6 explores some religious notions about love, miracles, divine revelation, and the possibility of a life beyond this life (or life after death). Chapter 7, finally, offers some practical guidelines on how to cultivate and practice philosophy of religion today.

At the end of this introduction and in the next six chapters I have included discussion questions for additional reflection. The questions are posed to stimulate further thought, rather than to test the reader's comprehension of the text. I regard the questions as *live* and not subject to routine, uniform responses that all well-informed readers (including those who are professional philosophers) would agree upon.

Discussion questions

What do you think are the limits (if any) of a respectful use of the Golden Rule or Good Samaritan precepts in philosophy? Do you believe there are some viewpoints or ways of reasoning that should be ruled out as off-limits? On my college campus, for example, there is zero tolerance for the advocacy of white supremacy, whether it arises from religious or secular points of view. Does a healthy tolerance of different philosophical views require an intolerance of some positions?

Critically consider the definition of religion proposed in this introduction. Would it allow some practices that are today not recognized as religions (such as voodoo), or perhaps some political movements or nation states in which there is deep reverence for powerful leaders, to count as religions? Consider also certain environmentalists who approach the natural world with reverence and awe, and contend that the experience of the natural world can be emancipatory, saving, illuminating, and transformative. There are even rituals celebrating the environment, such as Earth Day, recycling, and exercising good stewardship. The teachings and practices of the environmental movement derive from a wide range of sources, including not only the ecological sciences but also the works of figures such as Henry David Thoreau, John Muir, Rachel Carlson, and others, who are regarded as sages (not unlike saints). You may wish to consider the possibility that some elements of environmentalism resemble religious practices, in order to test the above definition of religion, but also to see whether you believe that construing the environmental movement as religious (or spiritual) is illuminating, desirable or undesirable.

1

Philosophy of Religion and Science

"Philosophy of religion," like philosophy of science, philosophy of art, and philosophy of economics, refers to what we call a *sub-field* or an *area of specialization* in the overall field or practice of philosophy. Like most fields you encounter in the world, there are various points of entry. I propose we enter philosophy of religion here by considering the relationship between religion and science. After all, our era is largely defined by science-based technology and, apart from some skeptics, science today is thought of by most people as a primary source of knowledge. What, then, is the relationship between religion and science? How do religious beliefs and practices compare with scientific beliefs and practices? To begin responding to these questions, consider the following statement on the subject from the National Academy of Sciences and Institute of Medicine (2008):

> Science and religion are based on different aspects of human experience. In science, explanations must be based on evidence drawn from examining the natural world. Scientifically based observations or experiments

that conflict with an explanation eventually must lead to modification or even abandonment of that explanation. Religious faith, in contrast, does not depend only on empirical evidence, is not necessarily modified in the face of conflicting evidence, and typically involves supernatural forces or entities. Because they are not a part of nature, supernatural entities cannot be investigated by science. In this sense, science and religion are separate and address aspects of human understanding in different ways. Attempts to pit science and religion against each other create controversy where none needs to exist.

This view of science and religion seems promising on many fronts. In the introduction it was observed that philosophical arguments are different from quarrels. If the above statement on science and religion is accurate, then it would imply minimal conflict between two dynamic aspects of what the Academy refers to as "human experience." In terms of the content of religion, I will challenge the Academy's use of the term "supernatural entities," but the quotation does seem to be correct in suggesting that the key elements of many religions neither admit of direct scientific investigation nor rest "only on empirical evidence." Neither God nor Allah nor Brahman (the divine as conceived of in Judaism, Christianity, Islam, and Hinduism) is a physical or material object or process. It seems, then, that the divine or the sacred, like many other elements in world religions (meditation, prayer, sin and forgiveness, deliverance from craving), can only be indirectly investigated by science. So, a neurologist might produce detailed studies of the brains of monks and nuns when they pray and meditate, and we can even do comparative studies of the health of those who practice a religion and those who do not, but it is very hard to conceive of how one would scientifically measure the role of God or Allah or Brahman or the Dao, and so on.

Despite the initial plausibility of the Academy's stance, however, I will suggest that it is problematic, beginning with a minor observation about terminology; specifically, the statement's reference to "supernatural forces or entities" that "are not part of nature." The term "supernatural" is not the standard term used to refer to God or the divine, probably, at least in part, because it refers not just to God or the divine, but also to the paranormal: poltergeists, ghosts, devils, witches, mediums, oracles, warlocks, séances, and so on, which are commonly thought to be matters of superstition. (For skeptics, the similarity of the terms *supernatural* and *superstitious* is properly suggestive.) The British philosopher Thomas Hobbes' use of the term "supernatural" fits this pattern when he refers to the supernatural nature of ghosts, witches, and other objects of superstition that are "repugnant to natural reason" (Hobbes 1998: chapter 46). In English, from the seventeenth century onward, the standard philosophical term to reference the belief that God exists is *theism* (from the Greek *theos*, for god/God). So, rather than the statement's reference to "supernatural forces or entities," a more charitable phrase would refer to how many world religions are theistic or, because some religions are non-theistic, involve some sacred reality (Nirvana, the Dao...) that is not directly, empirically measurable. Such a qualification would not rule out the possibility that the divine or the sacred could be experienced by persons insofar as experience can involve more than what would be standardly labeled as "empirical." Some of the relevant experiential data is available through the Religious Experience Resource Centre (RERC) at the University of Wales (formerly at Harris Manchester College, Oxford).

While traditional theistic traditions do not identify God with the natural world (God is not a planet or galaxy or force field, and so on), traditional theists hold that God is omnipresent or immanent throughout the cosmos; there is no place where God is not. On their view, God is not absent from space and time. That is why the following definition of the supernatural in Blackwell's *Dictionary of Philosophy* seems inappropriate or at least misleading in relation to theism:

> Supernatural beings exist above or beyond nature, where 'nature' is to be understood in a wide sense, to take in all of space and time and everything existing within that framework, i.e. the whole of the physical universe ... If scientists discover a new type of wave, a new force, a strange force in a remote galaxy, the very fact that it was there to be discovered makes it a natural phenomenon which may in due course be described in science textbooks. Supernatural beings run no risk of having their existence disclosed by scientific or everyday observation. (Mautner 1996: 416)

We will explore what might be meant when religions assert that God is present throughout space and time (Chapter 3), but an important point needs to be made here that even if it is rare for theists (or non-theistic thinkers) to suppose that God or the sacred can be the object of direct scientific examination, it is widely held, historically and today, that the sacred can be experienced (even in "everyday observation"), and that the recognition or denial of God is very much a matter of evidence. Consider, as an example, the evidence of evil in our world.

One of the strongest and most important objections to the reasonability of belief in the God of Judaism, Christianity, Islam, and theistic Hinduism is the evident amount of evil in the world. If there is an all-good, omnipresent, all-powerful, all-knowing Creator, why are there so many disastrous tragedies, from the premature death of children to the horrors of the Holocaust and the other massive atrocities of the twentieth century? To be sure, there are important responses that defend the rationality of believing in God's goodness in light of such events (and even arguments that such horrifying episodes may give us some reason to hope that the God of theism exists), but such objections and responses seem to require arguments that appeal to and access evidence. Granted, as has been noted, this evidence may go beyond what is narrowly defined as "empirical" (restricted to sensory observations), in the sense that one cannot measure evil the way one measures radiation, sea levels, or the temperature, but we do scientifically investigate suffering and death, birth defects as well as healthy births, humane collaborative activity, the practice of medicine, and so on. All this amounts to evidence that has a bearing on theistic religions and the non-theistic traditions that face up to the problem of evil.

In addition to arguments about the relevance of evil and goodness in assessing the evidence for and against religious beliefs, some philosophers (as noted earlier) consider the nature of religious experience itself as providing evidence for the divine. Some have also sought to assess the evidence for religious and secular views of reality in light of the contingent nature of the cosmos, its stable laws of nature, the emergence of consciousness, the nature of ethical values, and more.

One reason, however, for supporting the National Academy of Sciences' notion that religion and science do not overlap is the fact that, in the modern era, the natural sciences have bracketed reference to minds and the mental. That is, modern science has been concerned with a mind-independent physical world, whereas religions are concerned (primarily but not exclusively) with mind (feelings, emotions, thoughts, ideas, and so on) and the natural world in relation to our experience of life. The science of Kepler, Copernicus, Galileo, and Newton was carried out as an explicit study of the world without appeal to anything involving what today we would refer to as the mental or the psychological. So, Newton's laws of motion, concerning the attraction and repulsion of material objects, make no mention of how love or desire or emotional need might be required to explain the tendency of two material bodies to embrace romantically. Rather, explanations in modern science are all given in terms of force, motion, mass, and the like. As we shall observe later in this chapter, this exclusion of the mental or mind in scientific explanations gives rise to an important challenge that needs to be taken seriously in the philosophy of religion. But for now we need only note that the natural sciences at the beginning of the modern era deliberately did not appeal to what many scientists know to be true. That is, from Kepler through Newton and on into the early twentieth century, scientists themselves did not doubt the causal significance of minds; they simply did not include minds—their own or those of others—among the data they were studying. Interestingly, however, most of the early modern scientists believed that what they were studying was in some fashion made possible by the whole of the natural world (terrestrial and celestial) being created and sustained in existence by a Divine Mind, by an all-good, necessarily existing Creator. They had an overall or comprehensive worldview according to which science itself was reasonable and made sense. And indeed scientists today still have to have a kind of faith or trust in their methods, as well as a kind of faith or trust in a cosmos ordered such that those methods will prove effective and reliable. The earliest modern scientists thought such faith—a faith in what Einstein refers to as "the rationality and intelligibility of the world"—was reasonable because of their belief in the existence of God (Cain 2015: 42).

So, to return to the question raised at the outset of this chapter, I would argue that the National Academy's statement is misleading in suggesting that religious beliefs and practices are not sensitive to evidence, or not subject to modification in the face of counter-evidence. I suggest, instead, that both science and religion can be sensitive to evidence, though in the case of the latter the

evidence will tend to be more philosophical than empirical in a narrow sense. It is only because the natural
sciences bracket reference to minds and the mental, and
so do not directly speak to the life of religion, that there
is the appearance of non-conflict.

For the rest of the chapter, we will consider two elements in the science-religion relationship: first, an argument that the world of science itself might provide some
evidence for a religious belief or orientation to the
world; second, and conversely, a radical argument
appealing to science that might undermine the truth or
plausibility of most religions.

A cosmological argument for the natural world

The argument that follows is often labeled as a *cosmological argument*. It involves a line of reasoning with
deep roots going back to Plato and Aristotle, refined by
multiple Arabic philosophers, and defended today by
some (but by no means all) philosophers. In the version
I advance here, the starting point is that the cosmos as
disclosed in the sciences appears to exist contingently
as opposed to necessarily. "Contingent" here contrasts
with "necessary." Necessary truths cannot but be true,
such as 1+1=2. The latter proposition is necessarily true
for it turns out to be an identity statement. The number
2 simply is 1+1, so the identity turns out to be 1+1=1+1.
The logical law of identity (A is A, or *everything is itself*)
and the law of non-contradiction (A is not not-A) are
recognized by many philosophers as necessary or non-
contingent truths. There are indefinitely many necessary
truths, such as *there cannot exist more red spheres than
there are spheres*. Truths about the natural world do
not have this necessity. We can conclude that 1+1=2
without making any empirical observations whatsoever,
but we need to discover that water consists of oxygen
and hydrogen. Even the very existence of water is not

necessary. We can imagine a cosmos radically different from ours, with no water, no stable laws of nature, no planets or suns. That is why science involves discovery, experimentation, and observation.

In the sciences, explanations involve linking events with one another in causal relationships. In the philosophy of science this is a complex matter. According to some philosophers, explanations require identifying and linking laws of nature. Water boils at 212 degrees Fahrenheit at sea level because of the laws of nature involving hydrogen, oxygen, elevation, atmospheric pressure, and so on. According to others, the laws of nature are abstractions and the real causal explanations are to be found among particular objects and their properties and relations, the properties of molecules, atoms, and subatomic particles. In any case, whether we appeal to laws or to the properties of particular objects, our explanations take place within our cosmos, relating one set of causal events to others. So far, so good, as far as a science of the natural world goes.

But now, let us raise a question about the philosophy of science and the philosophy of the natural world. All scientific explanation takes place *within* the natural world. But what about an explanation for *the existence of the natural world itself and, therefore, for the practice of science?* Does explaining some contingent event, A, in terms of some other contingent event, B, reduce the contingency involved? In other words, can even a complete scientific explanation of the cosmos in terms of contingent events give us an answer to the question of *why there is a cosmos at all?* Or *why there is this cosmos rather than a different one?* I propose that it could not. Explaining contingent things and events in terms of other contingent things and events only expands the number of contingent things requiring an explanation. We naturally want some account of why our cosmos has the gravity it has (if gravity had been weaker, there would have been no galaxies, stars, or planets), and the explanation of such factors in terms of other contingent factors makes perfect sense. But here we are raising a question about the need to go beyond the contingent to account for contingency.

Before further developing a cosmological argument along these lines, let us first consider the concept of God as it appears in what are known as the Abrahamic religions—Judaism, Christianity, and Islam—as well as in theistic Hinduism. In these religions, God is believed to exist *necessarily*, not *contingently*. God exists in God's self, not as the creation of some greater being (a super-God) or force of nature. God is also not a mode of something more fundamental, the way a wave is a mode of the sea or a dance is a mode of movement. The nature of God in these religions is sometimes described in terms of God's very essence (what it is to be God) being identical with God's existence. In contrast, you and I have an essence—we are both human beings—but the very essence of being a human being is not existence, for our species did not always exist and, sadly, may come to an end some day. Human beings, and the cosmos as a whole, exist *contingently*; that is, they might not have existed at all. God's existence, however, is unconditional insofar as it does not depend upon any external conditions, whereas the cosmos and all it contains is conditional.

Theists hold that God is a *substantial reality*: a being not explainable in terms that are more fundamental than itself. God is without parts, that is, not an aggregate or compilation of things. Theists describe God as holy or sacred, a reality that is of unsurpassable greatness. God is therefore also thought of as perfectly good, beautiful, all-powerful (omnipotent), present everywhere (omnipresent), and all-knowing (omniscient). God is without origin and without end: everlasting or eternal. These latter terms are used to cover two distinguishable positions: some theists hold that God is temporal but without temporal beginning or end (God is everlasting), while others contend that God is not in time, but atemporally eternal (there is no temporal past, present, and future for God; God is, rather, the timeless creator of time). In virtue of God's awesome, transcendent attributes, God is worthy of worship and morally sovereign (worthy of obedience). In the Abrahamic tradition, God is manifested in human history, and God's nature and will is displayed in the tradition's sacred scriptures. Many (but not all) philosophers in this tradition have held that we have evidence of God both through revelation as well as through philosophical reflection on the nature of God and the cosmos. By their lights, the existence and continuation of the cosmos are due to the sustaining creativity of God, whose will it is that there be a good creation. And so we come back to the point raised earlier about evil in the cosmos. Theistic philosophers have offered reasons for us to believe in the goodness of the created order, notwithstanding the evident great evils.

Let us now resume our reflections on the natural world and science in relation to the cosmological argument we are developing here. If scientific explanations only explain one contingent event or thing in relation to another contingent thing, will we ever have an explanation of the whole cosmos or of why any cosmos exists at all? Arguably not. Consider two analogies. Imagine you see a light in a mirror. You might ask why there is such a light, and be given the answer that the light is reflected from another mirror. You ask about that mirror and are told that it comes from yet another mirror. It seems that to reach a satisfactory explanation for why there is any light at all you need to go outside the series to a source, for example the sun. In a second analogy, take a word of which you have no idea of its meaning: e.g. Omishimalag (a word I just made up). You ask for its meaning and are told Mishmortat (again a word I just invented), and so on and on in a series in which you are just given one-word terms but are never able to escape the series and point, for example, to a dog, thus defining the term by pointing to its referent (meaning). The cosmological line of reasoning presented here is that unless there is a causal power that is non-contingent and powerful enough to explain why there is a cosmos at all and why it should endure over time, you will not have a sufficient explanation of the cosmos itself.

The argument may be formalized as follows:

1. It is reasonable to explain events, seeking reasons for why they occur or don't occur, or for why some events occur rather than others.
2. It is reasonable to explain contingent things (objects, events, processes) in the cosmos in terms of other contingent things in the cosmos.
3. If the explanation of contingent things is given only in terms of other contingent things, we will not have an explanation of the cosmos itself (of why there is a cosmos at all, or why our particular cosmos exists rather than some other cosmos, or why the cosmos endures in existence).
4. We can explain the existence of the cosmos if we posit that its existence and continuation is due to the causal efficacy of a necessarily existing being.

Before considering objections and replies to this argument, it should be noted that even if you accept it, it does not follow that the powerful necessary cause of the cosmos is the God of the Abrahamic faiths. You would have a reason for thinking that there might be such a God, just as if you discover that there is life on another planet, you would have reason for thinking that there might be *intelligent* life on another planet. But the cosmological argument only gives us reason to believe that there is at least one necessary, sustaining creative cause, not that that cause is omniscient, all good, and so on. Still, if there is a necessary, non-contingent cause one would have reason to think there is more to the cosmos than what is disclosed in the natural sciences.

Let's consider two objections to the argument.

Objection one: What is the explanation for God or the necessary being? Doesn't the cosmological argument just push back the level of explanation to a "it just is"? If God just is, why not claim that the cosmos just is?

In reply, it is helpful to bear in mind the point just made: that while the argument provides a reason for thinking that there is a necessarily existing cause, it is not an all-out argument for the God of the Abrahamic faiths. A necessarily existing being is simply a being whose existence cannot be explained in terms of any other being or force or law or process. If a necessarily existing being were to be explicable in terms of some other force, it would not be necessary or non-contingent. A necessary being or truth simply is something that could not be otherwise. As Gary Gutting observes: "The explanation of everything contingent must be something that is not contingent; namely, something that not only exists but also cannot not exist; it must, that is, be necessary. If it weren't necessary, it would be contingent and so itself in need of explanation" (Gutting 2015: 98).

Objection two: Why not just accept that explanations of contingency in light of contingency are all that we are entitled to? Often, scientific accounts of events are all that we rely on and all that we believe we can rely on. If we have explained all the parts of an object and their interactions, haven't we explained the whole thing? Maybe there is no reason why the cosmos exists as a whole, and thus there is no "ultimate" reason why there is a cosmos at all.

A famous objection along these lines, advanced by Paul Edwards, proceeds by way of an analogy with explanations of a series of events in terms of other events. Edwards asks us to imagine a group of five Eskimos in New York City. We have an explanation for why each of the Eskimos are in the city: one is there for the climate, another because she is a detective investigating a crime, and so on. Once we have an explanation for why each Eskimo is in New York, it would be a mistake to ask why the group of Eskimos is there. "There is no group over and above the five members, and if we have explained why each of the five members is in New York we have ipso facto explained why the group is there" (Hospers 1997: 208).

Does the cosmological argument make this mistake? I do not think so. Explanations of members of a collection in terms of other members of the collection do not amount to an explanation of the set as a whole. The explanation of the Eskimos in terms of each other offers only a partial rather than an ultimate explanation of why there are any Eskimos at all. Gary Gutting notes how objections like Edwards' are unsuccessful even if the explanations go on to infinity:

> We can agree that there might be an infinite series of contingent explainers but still maintain that such an infinite series itself needs an explanation. We might, in effect, grant that there could be an infinite series of tortoises, each supporting the other—and the whole chain supporting the Earth—but still insist that there must be some explanation for why all those tortoises exist. That is, our argument will require that an infinite regress of contingent things must itself have an explanation. (Gutting 2015: 100–1)

Objection two reminds us that the cosmological argument as presented here is a philosophical rather than scientific argument. It is an argument to the effect that if explanations within the natural world make sense, then it also makes sense to ask for an explanation of the natural world itself. The objection becomes less plausible if we can form a richer understanding of the necessary cause that accounts for the very existence of the cosmos. It is here that we can appreciate how arguments for and against the existence of God are interwoven. Cosmological considerations are often, for example, related to considerations of goodness and purpose that come up in what are called *teleological arguments* (to be discussed in Chapter 4). In such arguments it is claimed that the apparent goodness and purposive nature of the cosmos provides us with one reason to believe that there is a good, purposive Creator.

So, if we have reason to believe that the notion of a necessarily existing cause of the cosmos makes sense, then we will see the cosmological argument as providing some reason for thinking there is such a being. Whereas if the concept of God or of a necessarily existing being can be shown to be confused or incoherent, then we have reason to resist the cosmological argument as well as the teleological argument. An analogy might be useful here. It may be that it is better to see arguments for or against belief in the existence of God as being more like the legs of a chair rather than links in a chain. A chain may only be as strong as its weakest link, but a chair might be supported by multiple legs of varying strength.

So far in this chapter I have proposed that the cosmological argument may provide *some reason* for thinking that there is more to the natural world than is disclosed in the natural sciences. How forceful this argument is remains to be seen (or is left for your assessment in light of references to further work in Chapter 7; for a recent development of the argument, see Pruss and Rasmussen 2018; O'Connor 2008). We will consider more arguments on this front in Chapters 4 and 5, but let us now consider a different argument that appeals to science, one which claims that the only real world is the world disclosed by the natural sciences.

An argument against religious traditions in the name of science

In contrast to the statement by the National Academy of Sciences with which we began this chapter, some philosophers adopt what might be called a warfare model of the relationship between science and religion. According to Steven Pinker, for example, science has shown the beliefs found in many religions to be false:

> To begin with, the findings of science entail that the belief systems of all the world's traditional religions and cultures—their theories of the origins of life, humans, and societies—are factually mistaken. We know, but our ancestors did not, that humans belong to a single species of African primate that developed agriculture, government, and writing late in its history. We know that our species is a tiny twig of a genealogical tree that embraces all living things and that emerged from prebiotic chemicals almost four billion years ago. (Pinker 2013)

We can also note that it would not be scientifically acceptable today to appeal to miracles or to direct acts of God. To many scientists, any supposed miracle would be a kind of defeat, an unacceptable mystery. This is why some philosophers of science propose that the sciences are *methodologically atheistic*. That is, while science itself does not pass judgment on whether or not God exists (even though some philosophers of science do), appealing to God's existence forms no part of its theories or investigations.

In my view, Pinker's position is overstated and it would be fairer to characterize the sciences as *methodologically agnostic* (simply taking no view on the question of God's existence) rather than atheistic (taking a position on the matter). Furthermore, as Michael Ruse has pointed out, Pinker's examples of what science has shown to be wrong seem unsubstantial:

> The arguments that are given for suggesting that science necessitates atheism are not convincing. There is no question that many of the claims of religion are no longer tenable in light of modern science. Adam and Eve, Noah's Flood, the sun stopping for Joshua, Jonah

and the whale, and much more. But more sophisticated Christians know that already. The thing is that these things are not all there is to religions, and many would say that they are far from the central claims of religion— God existing and being creator and having a special place for humans and so forth. (Ruse 2014: 74–5)

Ruse goes on to note that religions address the kind of concerns we have taken note of in considering the cosmological argument. It is worth pointing out that while he is defending the significance of religious ques- tions and the compatibility of religion and science, Ruse himself is an atheist. As such, his position is less prey to the charge that he is engaged in Christian apologetics. Because of the importance of the issues and the clarity of Ruse's writing, I will cite the relevant passage at length:

> Why is there something rather than nothing? What is the purpose of it all? And (somewhat more controversially) what are the basic foundations of morality and what is sentience? Science takes the world as given. Science sees no ultimate purpose to reality ... I would say that as science does not speak to these issues, I see no reason why the religious person should not offer answers. They cannot be scientific answers. They must be religious answers—answers that will involve a God or gods. There is something rather than nothing because a good God created from love out of nothing. The purpose of it all is to find eternal bliss with the Creator. Morality is a function of God's will; it is doing what He wants us to do. Sentience is that by which we realize that we are made in God's image. We humans are not just any old kind of organism. This does not mean that the religious answers are beyond criticism, but they must be answered on philosophical or theological grounds and not simply because they are not scientific. (Ruse 2014: 76)

Ruse has rightly observed that Pinker's examples fail to strike at the core of religious beliefs in terms of what is of foundational importance. While he rebuts Pinker's argument against theistic religions in light of science, I would suggest that a forceful defense of non-theistic religions along the lines Ruse proposes is also possible. (For a fuller exploration of this debate see Abraham and Aquino 2017.)

Let us now turn to an even more radical case against religious beliefs and practices involving an appeal to science. Some philosophers contend that the natural sciences—physics, chemistry, and biology—offer the ultimate and only explanation of reality. As such, we should limit our beliefs to what is disclosed in the physical sciences. Daniel Dennett is a philosopher who holds this position:

> There is only one sort of stuff, namely matter—the physical stuff of physics, chemistry and physiology— and the mind is somehow nothing but a physical phenomenon. In short, the mind is the brain ... we can (in principle!) account for every mental phenomenon using the same physical principles, laws, and raw materials that suffice to explain radioactivity, continental drift, photosynthesis, reproduction, nutrition, and growth. (Dennett 1991: 33)

Dennett describes himself as a behaviorist. Behaviorists do not appeal to subjective states like beliefs and desires in explaining behavior. In fact, Dennett is highly skeptical that consciousness is a basic property of reality, rather than a mere appearance.

> My "behaviorism" ... is the behaviorism of science. Meteorology is behavioristic in this sense, and so is chemistry, and physics and geology and astronomy. When you achieve a theory and explain all meteorological behavior, you get to declare victory, you've finished the task, because that's all there is to explain. (Papineau and Dennett 2017: 16)

Cosmological explanations on this view are out of luck: the natural sciences are the final arbiter of what we can know, and insofar as religions posit that which goes beyond science, they are in jeopardy.

There is at least one big problem with Dennett's position. His worldview is very much in line with the meth odological commitment to bracket matters of mind and the mental in explanations. Thus, there is no recourse to explaining things in terms of desires, ideas, passions, emotions, and so on. Dennett assumes, instead, that we have a clear concept of explanations not involving mind. But it is one thing to bracket the mind in terms of explaining continental drift, and so on, but quite another to do so in explaining, for example, why I am writing this book and why you are reading it. It seems as though our ordinary lives are suffused with accounts of what occurs that are thoroughly mental or psycho-logical. Indeed, it seems very hard to believe that there could be science at all without scientists, and scientists are persons with experiences, observations, ideas and theories, thoughts and emotions. Rather than assum-ing the primacy of mind-independent explanations, I would suggest that we necessarily have a clearer grasp of that which involves the mind—thinking, conceiving, believing, observing, experiencing, and so on. As such, we cannot even understand Dennett's claims without a commitment to the fact that we understand concepts and ideas and their interrelationships, such as the idea of a law of nature, the idea of continental drift, and so on. As Linda Zagzebski notes, in order for Dennett or anyone else to claim to understand what they are propos-ing, including for scientists to claim to understand their science, the existence of consciousness must be affirmed: "Understanding is a state in which I am directly aware of the object of my understanding, and conscious trans-parency is a criterion for understanding" (Zagzebski 2001: 247). You cannot have conscious transparency, or lucid understanding, without being conscious. Given this essential primacy of the understanding and other mental states, both in science and in life as a whole,

Dennett's behavioristic effort to reject the mental and rely only on the natural sciences cannot succeed.

In short, Dennett's behaviorism undermines itself. The only explanations he countenances are those that do not involve reasons, desires, ideas, conscious understanding, etc., but the sciences he appeals to essentially involve reasons, desires, ideas, and conscious understanding. Moreover, his claims only make sense if we are confident of our explanations in terms of reasons, ideas, thoughts, and so on. Any effort to advance the authority of science over other forms of inquiry will require a philosophy of science and of the cosmos which justifies science. As Roger Trigg points out: "Because science is a human practice and needs justification, it must depend on a wider understanding of a reason that can provide a rational basis for some confidence in science as a means to truth" (Trigg 2015: xi).

Dennett also adopts a line of reasoning similar to the one we reached in relation to the cosmological argument. Earlier it was suggested that if positing a necessarily existing Creator of the contingent cosmos ran afoul of philosophical problems, then we might have a reason for rejecting the argument, just as we would have reasons to favor it if we can give a fuller account of a necessary cause (perhaps employing a teleological or other theistic argument). Dennett has long held that the only alternative to his eliminative approach to the mental would be some form of dualism. "Dualism" is the standard term for the view that the mind or the mental is not the same thing as the physical or material. Dennett believes that dualism should be avoided at all costs, because it would leave us with a bifurcation between what is evident in the physical world and what is mysterious.

It would be too much in this chapter to take on the case for and against dualism. In Chapters 5 and 6 some reasons are advanced for not identifying conscious experience with our brains and other bodily things and processes. There I resist using the term *dualism*, which suggests there are just two kinds of things, preferring instead the term *pluralism* (the view that there are many kinds of things). But here I will simply note that today contemporary science seems to leave us with a bewildering concept of what counts as physical. Some philosophers who insist on the open-ended, indeterminate nature of the physical world, such as Galen Strawson and Noam Chomsky, are not friends of dualism, but their insistence on our lack of a clear concept of what is physical should give pause to those persuaded by Dennett's suggestion that we have a problem-free concept of the physical. As Chomsky says, "the notion of 'the physical world' is open and evolving" (Chomsky 1980: 5). Much earlier, Bertrand Russell observed that contemporary physics has blown away any "common sense" grasp of matter: "Matter has become as ghostly as anything in a spiritualist séance" (Russell 1927: 78; for two excellent books addressing the philosophy of science and religion, see Stenmark 2004 and Ellis 2014).

I will return to topics of the mental and physical in Chapters 5 and 6. The aim of this first chapter has been to suggest that the sciences and religion can be compatible; in fact, there is a religiously significant cosmological argument that, if successful, supports the nature and practice of science. Moreover, there is some reason, or so I have argued, to be open to truths beyond what is explicitly recognized in the natural sciences alone. I propose, therefore, that we should be open to the reality of experience, subjectivity, feelings, and so on. In the next chapter, we will look in more detail at the experiences and ideas that take shape in the context of world religions.

Discussion questions

Some philosophers have claimed that simplicity is a mark of the truth. Should the view that only the natural world exists have priority due to its simplicity, over the belief that the natural world is the creation of God?

One objection against the cosmological argument is that we have readily available evidence of contingent events explaining the occurrence of other contingent events, but no evidence of such events being explained through the causation of a necessarily existing being. Consider this reply: We do have evidence of contingent events being explained by necessary realities. For example, it is a contingent matter that you and I exist and that we have mathematical abilities. But it is not a contingent matter that when we are asked which is the smallest perfect number, we reply that it is 6. A perfect number is an even number equal to the sum of its divisors, including 1 but not including itself. Six is the smallest possible such number, being equal to 3+2+1. The latter is a necessary truth, and a complete explanation of why we identify 6 as the smallest perfect number is because we grasp this necessary truth. Hence it is not the case that we are unfamiliar with necessary realities that have a causal role in our contingent world. What do you think?

It has been argued in this chapter that we have a clearer understanding of what may be termed the mental than we do of material or physical objects and events that are independent of the mind. Might this be reversed? We can answer questions about what water is made up of (H_2O), but can we answer questions about what makes up ideas, experiences, thinking, and so on?

2

Philosophy of Religion and the Meaning of Life

Questions about the meaning of something (what is the meaning of what you are doing right now?) are often questions about what is true (it is true you are reading this) and about its significance (you are reading this book because you wish to explore the philosophy of religion). If we ask about the meaning of life, we might at first find this too ambitious and puzzling. But if we understand the phrase "the meaning of life" broadly enough, then, in reflective moments, we do assume that our lives have multiple meanings in the pursuit of things we value—friendships, family, loyalties, happiness, the well-being of others, our goals in terms of our careers, commitments, and so on—and all of this bears on how our lives are connected to the larger, cosmic context. Are we the result of random causal forces with no prevision or purpose? Or are we made in the image of a divine Creator-God? Are we called to recognize that there is no God but Allah and Mohammad is his prophet? Might it be that our pursuit of our desires is the root of suffering and we are in need of the wisdom of the Buddha? Exploring the great world religions is an important way to engage with such large questions.

Before getting underway with comparing the answers to such questions, we should note that we have some reason to resist thinking that the meaning of our lives is an entirely subjective matter. After all, I might think that the meaning of my life is largely a matter of my being a generous, compassionate, conscientious professor, whereas (alas) it could turn out that I am hopelessly narcissistic, selfish, and a reprehensible obstacle to my students' education, routinely breaking the eleventh commandment of Thou shalt not be boring. I do not deny that subjectivity needs to be part of our understanding of the meaning of our lives; if I am earnestly trying to excel as a professor then it is at least true that I am trying to be such, even if I fail.

In terms of how religious worldviews might impact the meaning of our lives, let us begin with the Abrahamic faiths, and then turn to Hinduism and Buddhism.

The meaning of life according to the Abrahamic religions

Judaism, Christianity, and Islam are called *Abrahamic* because they trace their history back to the Hebrew patriarch Abraham (often dated to the twentieth or twenty-first century BCE). All three religions see themselves as rooted in Abrahamic faith, as displayed in the Hebrew Bible, the Christian Old Testament (essentially the Hebrew Bible) and New Testament, and the Qur'an. As noted in Chapter 1, "theism" has been the common term in English to refer to their central concept of God since the seventeenth century. According to the classical forms of these theistic faiths, God is the one God who created and sustains the cosmos. As such, they are *monotheistic* as opposed to *polytheistic*. According to the Abrahamic traditions, the cosmos was either created by God out of nothing (*ex nihilo*), or it has always existed, but its existence depends upon God's sustaining, creative will (some Islamic philosophers have taken the latter position, but the great majority of philosophers in all three traditions have held that the cosmos had a beginning in time). "Creation out of nothing" entails that God did not create the cosmos by shaping anything external to God. The cosmos depends upon God's conserving, continuous will in the way light depends upon a source, or a song depends upon a singer. If the source of the light goes out or the singer stops singing, the light and the song cease. Traditionally, the Creation is not thought of as something that an agent might fashion and then abandon; the idea that God might make Creation and then neglect it, the way a person might make a machine and then abandon it, is utterly foreign to theism. If theism is true, then no contingently created reality can persist in being without God's continuous sustaining power.

Arguably, the most important attribute of God in the Abrahamic traditions is *goodness*. The idea that God is not good, or the fundamental source of goodness, would be akin to the idea of a square circle—an utter contradiction. Theists in these traditions do, however, differ on some of the divine attributes. Some, for example, claim that God knows all future events with certainty, whereas others argue that no being (including God) can have such knowledge. Some theists believe that God transcends both space and time altogether, while others hold that God pervades the spatial world and is temporal—there is a before, during, and after for God. We will consider some of these differences in more detail in Chapter 3. But it is largely in their views of God's special revelation that the three monotheistic traditions diverge.

In Judaism, God's principal manifestation was in leading the people of Israel out of bondage in Egypt to the Promised Land (Canaan), as recounted in the book of Exodus. This "saving event" is commemorated perennially in the yearly observation of Passover. The Judaic tradition places enormous value on community life, a life displayed in the Hebrew Bible as a covenant between God and the people of Israel. The more traditional representatives of Judaism, especially the Orthodox, adopt a strict reading of what they take to be the historic meaning of the Hebrew scripture as secured in the early stages of its formation. Other groups, like the Conservative and Reformed, treat scripture as authoritative but do not subscribe to a specific, historically defined interpretation of that scripture. Although there is some lively disagreement about the extent to which Judaism affirms an afterlife for individuals, historically, central elements of later Judaism have included such an affirmation. This becomes more apparent in later Hebrew scriptures, such as the book of Ezekiel, and in the work of the famous medieval Jewish philosopher Maimonides.

Christians accept the Hebrew scriptures and Judaism's understanding of God's action in history, but expand it in holding that God became incarnate as Jesus Christ. Christ is understood as a person who has both divine and human natures, and whose birth, life, teaching, miracles, suffering, death, and resurrection are the principal means by which God delivers Creation from sin (moral and spiritual evil) and devastation. As part of its teaching about the incarnation, Christianity holds that while God is one, God is constituted by three persons in a supreme, singular unity called the trinity (to be discussed briefly in Chapter 3). Traditional Christianity asserts that through God's loving mercy and justice, individual persons are not annihilated at death, but either enjoy an afterlife in heaven or endure one in hell. Some Christians have been and are *universalists*, holding that ultimately God will triumph over evil and there will be universal salvation for all, though a greater part of the tradition holds that God will not violate the free will of creatures and that if individuals seek to reject God, then they will be everlastingly separated from God.

Some unity of Christian belief and practice was gradually achieved in the course of developing the various creeds that defined Christian faith in formal terms. The word "creed" comes from the Latin *credo*, "I believe," with which the creeds used in worship traditionally began. The Nicene Creed, most of which was written and approved in the third century, is the most famous and widely shared of these. At the heart of traditional Christianity are the initiation ritual of baptism and the rite of the Eucharist, which re-enacts or recalls Christ's self-offering through sharing blessed bread and wine, commonly called *communion* or *mass*. What unity Christianity achieved was broken, however, in the eleventh century with the split between Western (now the Catholic Church) and Eastern Christianity (now the Orthodox Churches), and broken again in the sixteenth century with a split between the Roman Catholic Church and the churches of the Reformation. Many denominations emerged after the Reformation, including the Anglican, Baptist, Lutheran, Methodist, and Presbyterian Churches. Since the middle of the twentieth century, greater unity between Christian communities has been pursued with some success. Some Christians treat the Bible as infallible and inerrant in its original form, while others treat it as authoritative and inspired but not free from historical error or fallible human influence.

Islam traces its roots back to Judaism and Christianity, acknowledging a common, Abrahamic past. Islamic teaching was forged by the Prophet Mohammed (570–632), who proclaimed a radical monotheism that explicitly repudiated both the polytheism of his time and the Christian understanding of the incarnation and the trinity. According to tradition, Islam's holy book the Qur'an (from *Qu'ra* for "to recite" or "to read") was received by Mohammed, who dictated this revelation of Allah (Arabic for "God") as revealed to him by the Archangel Gabriel. The Qur'an is thus taken to be

God's very speech. Central to Islam is the sovereignty of Allah, his providential control of the cosmos, and the importance of living justly and compassionately, following a set practice of prayer, worship, and pilgrimage.

A follower of Islam is called a Muslim, an Arabic term for "one who submits," since a Muslim submits to God. The Five Pillars of Islam are: reciting the Islamic creed, praying five times a day while facing Mecca, alms-giving, fasting during Ramadan (the ninth month of the Muslim calendar), and making a pilgrimage to Mecca. The two largest branches of Islam are the Sunnis and Shi'ites, the result of a split early in the history of Islam over a disagreement about who would succeed Mohammed. Sunnis comprise the vast majority of Muslims. Shi'ites put greater stress on the continuing revelation of God beyond the Qur'an as revealed in the authoritative teachings of the *imam* (holy successors who inherit Mohammed's "spiritual abilities"), the *mujtahidun* ("doctors of the law"), and other agents. Like Christianity, Islam proclaims that a loving, merciful, and just God does not annihilate an individual at death, but provides either heaven or hell.

Arguably, the truth of any one of these Abrahamic faiths would entail the truth of many of the beliefs of the others. For example, if Islam is true, much (but not all) of the history of God's covenant with the Jewish people is affirmed, and Jesus is acknowledged as a holy prophet of God. Moreover, all three faiths affirm that we live in a cosmos created and conserved in being by a holy, awesome God.

The meaning of life in light of Hinduism and Buddhism

While Judaism, Christianity, and Islam originated in the Near East, the two other major world religions, Hinduism and Buddhism, originated in Asia.

Hinduism is so diverse that it is difficult to use the term as an umbrella category, even to designate a host of interconnected ideas and traditions. "Hindu" is a Persian term referring to the various people and tradi tions that have flourished in the Indian subcontinent, going back to before the second millennium BCE. The most common feature of what is considered Hinduism is reverence for the Vedic scriptures, a rich collection of work, some of it highly philosophical, especially the Upanishads (written between 800 and 500 BCE). Unlike the three monotheistic religions, Hinduism does not look back to a singular historical figure such as Abraham.

According to Advaita Vedanta—a strand of Hinduism that has received a great deal of attention from Western philosophers in this and the last century—the world of space and time is ultimately illusory. The world is *Maya* (literally "illusion"). It appears to us to consist of diverse objects because of our ignorance. Behind the diverse objects and forms we observe in what may be called the phenomenal or apparent world, there is the formless, impersonal reality of Brahman. The Advaita school's principal aim is the rejection of this duality ("Advaita" comes from the Sanskrit term for "non-duality"). Brahman alone is ultimately real. This position is often called *monism* (from the Greek *monus* or "single") or *pantheism* ("God is everything"). Shankara (788–820) was one of the greatest teachers of this tradition within Hinduism. In his *Crest-Jewel of Discrimination* he explained that "Brahman alone is real. There is none but He. When He is known as the supreme reality there is no other existence but Brahman" (Shankara 1970: 82). "In dream," he wrote in the same book, "the mind creates by its own power a complete universe of subject and object. The waking state [too] is only a prolonged dream. The phenomenal universe exists in the mind" (1970: 71).

Other theistic strands of Hinduism construe the divine as personal, all-good, powerful, knowing, creative, loving, and so on. Theistic elements may be seen, for example, in the *Bhagavad Gita* (sixth century BCE) and its teaching about the love of God. Some of its breathtaking passages about Krishna's divine manifestation even seem similar to the great passages in the Gospel of John, where Christ proclaims or implies his divinity or divine calling. The philosopher Muidhva (c.1238–c.1317) is one of the better known theistic representatives of Hinduism.

Popular Hindu practice also includes a rich polytheism, and for this reason Hinduism has been called the religion of 330 million gods. The recognition and honor paid to these gods are sometimes absorbed into Brahman worship, as the gods are understood to be so many manifestations of the one true reality.

Whether their religion takes a monist or theistic form, many Hindus believe that a trinity of Brahma, Vishnu, and Shiva is the cardinal, supreme manifestation of Brahman. Brahma is the creator of the world, Vishnu its sustainer—manifested in the world as Krishna and Rama, incarnations or avatars (Sanskrit for "one who descends") who instruct and enlighten—and Shiva the destroyer.

Most Hindus believe in reincarnation. The soul migrates through different lives, according to the principles of *karma* (Sanskrit for "deed" or "action"), or the moral consequences of one's actions. The final consummation or enlightenment is *moksha* (or release) from *samsara*, the material cycle of birth and rebirth. In Hinduism's monist forms, liberation comes from overcoming the dualism of Brahman and the individual self or soul (*atman*, "breath"), and sometimes from merging into a transcendental self with which all other selves are identical. *Karma* is often associated with, and believed to be a chief justification for, a strict social caste system. Not all Hindus support such a system, and many Hindu reformers in the modern era have argued for its abolition.

Hinduism also has a legacy of inclusive spirituality. It understands other religions as different ways to enlightened unity with Brahman. In the *Bhagavad Gita*, Krishna declares:

> If any worshipper do reverence with
> faith to any God whatever,
> I make his faith firm,
> and in that faith he reverences his
> god,
> and gains his desires,
> for it is I who bestow them. (vii. 21–2)

Hinduism has also absorbed some of the teachings and narratives of Buddhism, as well as assimilating Christian elements, especially since British colonialism, with Jesus being seen as the tenth avatar of Vishnu. Although Hinduism and Islam have sometimes been in painful conflict, there have been instances of tolerance and collaboration. One of the aims of Sikhism, a six-teenth-century reform movement within Hinduism, was to bring together Hindus and Muslims.

Buddhism emerged from Hinduism, tracing its origin to Gautama Sakyamuni, who lived in northern India sometime between the sixth and fourth centuries BCE and came to be known as the Buddha ("Enlightened One"). His teaching centers on The Four Noble Truths: 1) life is full of suffering, pain, and misery (*dukka*); 2) the origin of suffering is in desire (*tanha*); 3) the extinc-tion of suffering can be brought about by the extinction of desire; and 4) the way to extinguish desire is by fol-lowing the Noble Eightfold Path. The Eightfold Path consists of right understanding; right aspirations or atti-tudes; right speech; right conduct; right livelihood; right effort; mindfulness; and contemplation or composure.

Early Buddhist teaching tended to be non-theistic, underscoring instead the absence of the self (*anatta*) and the impermanence of life. In its earliest forms, Buddhism did not have a developed metaphysics (a theory of the structure of reality, the nature of space, time, and so on), but did include belief in reincarnation, skepticism about the substantial nature of persons existing over time, and either a denial of the existence of Brahman or the treatment of Brahman as inconsequential. This is its clearest departure from Hinduism. In Buddhism, the goal of the religious life is *Nirvana*, a transformation of human consciousness that involves the shedding of the illusion of selfhood.

Schools of Buddhism include Theravada, the oldest and strictest in terms of promoting the importance of monastic life; Mahayana, which emerged later, placing less emphasis on monastic vocation and displaying less resistance to Hindu themes; Pure Land Buddhism in India and Central Asia; and Zen, which originated in China but spread throughout Asia and is popular in parts of the United States today.

The meaning of our lives

I would contend that the truths contained in these religious ways of thinking about the world (along with other traditions such as Daoism, Confucianism, Jainism, and others) should impact on our understanding of the meaning of life, and of our own lives in particular. Let us explore this in the context of four objections and replies.

Objection one: Why think that the meaning of a person's life depends on things that are supposed to be "true" independently of a person's actual beliefs and practices? If someone thinks they are happy, it seems arrogant to claim that, "deep down," they really are not. If we are not in a position to know with certainty which, if any, religion is true, then it seems pointless to concern oneself with determining which religious view of reality seems more reasonable. After all, if expert philosophers disagree over the matter, why trust one's own reasoning?

Reply: This first objection is forceful. To some extent, what one actually thinks and feels is very much what would naturally be thought of as constituting the meaning of one's life. If I am depressed then I am depressed, regardless of what anyone else might say. But it is very difficult to limit our understanding of our identity to just what we think and feel about ourselves. To go back to the case mentioned at the outset of this chapter, I may think I am generous and loving when it turns out I am actually vain and manipulative. Just as our words do not necessarily mean what we think they mean—you may intend to compliment someone when actually you are insulting them—it may be that what we think of as the meaning of who we are may not match reality. As such, it is hard to limit our identity only to what we think about ourselves and not take into account whether our thoughts are true or not. As an illustration, consider how one's beliefs about one's surroundings may impact one's grasp of the meaning of what is taking place. In a classroom, two of my students appeared to be engaged in a fierce fight. I was shocked, and momentarily paralyzed about what to do. But it soon became clear that the fight was mere play; they had, so I later learned, put on a very convincing theatrical act in order to provide me with a setting in which I could break up a fight and bring about reconciliation. The whole thing was performed under the mantle of friendship rather than hostility. Likewise, arguably, the reality and significance of the world around us may be quite ambiguous or have multiple possible meanings: sometimes it appears that we live in a cosmos created and sustained by a Creator, sometimes the cosmos appears to some of us to be unguided, random, and without purpose. Perhaps sometimes it appears that we are in a cycle of suffering and craving and that the Buddha points the way to enlightenment. In determining which of these visions (among others) is right we are given alternative understandings of who we are and what we are facing.

The objection makes the charge of arrogance, but questions of arrogance need not come up when discussing the meaning of life—whether one's own or someone else's. It may even be that appreciating that the meaning of one's own life extends beyond one's own viewpoint is liberating. To give a personal example: for years I claimed to love what I do—teaching at St. Olaf College. However, I did not truly know this until I had a job offer from a different school, and decided to stay at St. Olaf. It took a dramatic event and process for me to recognize what I really valued. I would suggest that this is often the case in relation to love and friendship. Sometimes we don't actually know who or what we love or who our friends are until some event arises that calls for loyalty and energy. So, discussing the meaning of one's loves and values can itself be a valuable experience and not a matter of disdain or arrogance.

The objection also raises the subject of disagreements between "experts." Here I would argue that while such disagreements on religious (and other) worldviews are disconcerting, this may not be enough to get us off the hook in terms of taking our own time to consider the great religions described in this chapter (and others) from a secular perspective. There have been times in the history of culture when "experts" have legitimated what we now know to be racist and sexist beliefs. Sometimes, having a justified belief in terms of ethics or religion is a matter in which the so-called "non-experts" might be better placed to recognize the truth. In Ancient Greece, for example, the leading experts got it wrong about slavery—Plato and Aristotle deemed it legitimate—whereas the rogue, anti-establishment philosopher, Diogenes of Sinope, recognized the illicit nature of enslavement.

Objection two: The five world religions all seem different, but what if they turn out to be different ways of approaching the same truth or sacred reality? The philosopher John Hick (1989) famously argued that all world religions are different points of view or perspectives on what he referred to as the Real. The Real is a supremely good, sacred reality that beckons us to leave behind our self-centered existence and live generously for the well-being of others. If Hick is correct, then the exploration of the meaning of life need not involve a choice between the great world religions; they all converge on the same end, the Real.

Reply: We need to appreciate that there is indeed a great deal of mutual agreement among the different religious traditions. So much so that there have been efforts on the part of virtually all world religious leaders to find a common ground for addressing the injustices in the world. The World Council of Religious Leaders, for instance, "aims to serve as a model and guide for the creation of a community of world religions ... [b]y promoting the universal human values shared by all religious traditions and by uniting the human community for times of world prayer and meditation." Whether we agree with Hick on the unified object of the different world religions, this collaborative, multi-religious pursuit of justice and concord is deeply admirable.

Nevertheless, there are some divergences among the world religions that are difficult to process in terms of reducing them to different viewpoints on the same reality. As noted earlier in the chapter, Christians affirm the incarnation and the trinity, whereas both are denied in Judaism and Islam. Hindus affirm the reality of Brahman, whereas this is denied by Buddhists. Still, there are some subtle as well as major agreements. While Jews and Muslims deny the incarnation in which Jesus of Nazareth is both divine and human, they do affirm something like an incarnation in which the eternal divine enters into contact with humans. For observant Jews, wisdom is often depicted as a divine presence among the people (see Proverbs 1 and 8, for example).

Wisdom is believed to be with God and yet enters into the world. For Muslims, the Qur'an is the eternal word of God and yet it enters into time. There is a sense, then, in which all three Abrahamic faiths recognize some manifestation of the divine in the world.

Objection three: Why bother with exploring the meaning of life in a religious context when religion is the source of so much conflict and violence in the world?

Reply: Events such as the terrorist attack of 9/11 and the atrocities committed by ISIS have led some of us to forget that the worst violence in recent history was not at all motivated by religious belief. Consider the genocides and massacres perpetrated by Stalin in the Soviet Union, Leopold II in Belgium, Hitler throughout Europe, Mao Zedong in China, Pol Pot in Cambodia, and Saddam Hussein in Iraq, among others. Religion is not the primary motive for violence, but a secondary or even tertiary motive that magnifies more fundamental drives having to do with our very human disposition to favor self and kin and to form cooperatives that distinguish between in-groups and out-groups. I believe Kelly Clark is correct to suggest that:

(1) Violence almost always originates in threats to self, kin and tribe (people typically fight over land, kin and food).
(2) Threats to self-kin-tribe instinctively elicit fight or flight responses.
(3) Religion, like other tribal markers, is not a primary cause of violence.
(4) While tribal markers make identification of in-group (family, friend) and out-group (competitor, enemy) easier, they are not the primary motive in violence. (Clark 2017: 21)

As Clark observes, there is a pervasive human tendency to protect oneself and one's family. We then identify with larger groups, whether a tribe or a non-related community, and seek to protect them through force.

We tend to regard others not aligned with our group as potentially hostile and deserving suspicion and distrust.

In his excellent book, *Is Religion Dangerous?*, Keith Ward similarly argues that "What makes beliefs evil is not religion, but hatred, ignorance, the will to power, and indifference to others" (Ward 2007: 35). In a sense, both Clark and Ward endorse Machiavelli's observation that if you wish to do evil, then, from a prudential point of view, it is best carried out with the appearance of morality and religion: "The distortion of evil to make it appear good is one of the first tricks of the successfully evil. So religion is one of the main weapons in the armoury of evil" (Ward 2007: 54).

Returning to the objection, it may be granted that some violence in the world today does appear to be motivated by extreme religious views. Terrorists kill people, shouting "Allahu Akbar." Arguably, however, this violence is most often motivated by a sense of injustice, alienation, or estrangement, or even by a desire to be heroic (to make one's life significant), in which religion plays no primary role. More positively, I would suggest that if one takes a deeper look at world religions, including Islam, one will find profound teachings about love, compassion, mercy, justice. Considering the meaning of one's life in relation to these teachings can open us up to challenging virtues. We will return to some of these issues in Chapter 6.

Objection four: Wouldn't a better, more humble approach to the great world religions be to assume a state of reverent agnosticism, admitting that one does not know which path is the correct one?

Reply: Humility is indeed a preeminent virtue, and if one is honestly uncertain about which religion (if any) offers a plausible view of reality and value, then agnosticism seems altogether fitting. I would only add two qualifications. First, agnosticism does not rule out religious commitment and practice. One may practice a religion without claiming to know it is true. In fact, to some extent, I am a religious practitioner who does not claim to know with certainty that the religion I participate in is fundamentally true. I believe it to be, with some reason, but I also believe I could be mistaken. Second, I would suggest that an agnosticism that has resulted from inquiry—in which one carefully considers the case for different worldviews—is more admirable than one which is the result of no inquiry at all. The stakes in terms of the meaning of one's life are, in my view, pretty high. Arguably, if you love your life and the lives of others, it is desirable to consider some of the big questions to the fullest extent that one is able: Could it be that Buddha is correct and that suffering is the result of craving? Could we all share an identity with Atman and, ultimately, with Brahman? Might it be the case that we are made in the image of God?

In this chapter, we have looked at how engaging with world religions philosophically can play an important role in exploring the meaning of life. In the next chapter, we will consider further the philosophy of God and of the sacred.

Discussion questions

What if we think of the different world religions, not so much as true or false, but as narratives or frameworks that instill awe, or are beautiful, or enable us to live more fully? Arguably, our lives can be shaped by enriching works of imagination (for me, *The Lord of the Rings*), even though we know such works are not descriptive of the real world. Might something similar be true of religion? (See Wettstein 2012 for a development of this position.)

How far can disagreement go? In order to disagree on a topic, doesn't there have to be some significant agreement already in place? If we entirely differ in our understanding of God, and you claim God exists, and I claim God does not exist, might it be the case that we are not really engaged in a disagreement at all?

What about intermixing religions? There was a famous moment in the life of Gandhi, vividly portrayed in the 1982 film *Gandhi*. He is undertaking a fast to try to end the violence between Muslims and Hindus. A member of a Hindu death-squad bursts into where Gandhi is staying and urges him to eat, so breaking the fast. Gandhi refuses. The man then confesses to Gandhi that he is in hell. Gandhi asks him why this is so. The man reports that he has killed a Muslim boy the same age as his son, because his own son had been killed by a Muslim. Gandhi tells the man that he knows a way out of hell. He tells him to find a Muslim boy the same age as his son, and to raise the boy as a Muslim. This is an extraordinary exchange, perhaps bringing the man to a kind of penance for his crime, and also compelling or inviting him to empathize with Muslims. While dramatic, this case may make for interesting reflection. If you were a Hindu and honestly believed that Islam is false, would this put you in an awkward position, being asked to raise a child in a religious faith that you thought was mistaken?

When do different religions worship the same God and how would this be determined? Imagine that Hinduism is true and that Jesus of Nazareth is not the unique incarnation of God but an avatar of Vishnu. In this case, would a Christian actually be worshiping, without knowing it, a Hindu divinity?

3

Divine Attributes

Reflection on divine attributes has been an extraordinary source of philosophical work over the centuries, and continues to be so today. This work incorporates thought on the nature of values, the mental and the physical, power, creativity, purposive action, knowledge, time, meaning, and the very concept of being a person.

In this chapter we will consider the following attributes: perfection and being worthy of worship; divine necessity; incorporeality; omnipotence; omniscience; and being eternal or everlasting. At the end of the chapter, we will look at some attributes of the divine that go beyond classical theism.

Perfection and being worthy of worship

In the Abrahamic faiths God is understood to be unsurpassable in excellence. There is no greater, more valuable being than God. In the words of the medieval philosophical theologian Anselm, God is that being greater than which nothing can be conceived. It is this notion of maximal greatness that has directed significant human thought on God. One reason for thinking God is omniscient or all-knowing is that knowledge is linked to goodness or greatness. Values are sometimes comparable or commensurate, but sometimes not. We would be puzzled if we were asked to compare certain values— which is better, the value of friendship or the value of art? In the case of the divine, Anselmians have thought of God as having the greatest set of compossible properties. Two properties are compossible when it is possible for a single being to instantiate both; for example, if theism is true, then the attributes of omniscience and omnipotence are compossible. One concern running through philosophical work on the divine attributes is the extent to which they are compossible. Is it possible, as the Anselmians claim, for God (or a single being) to be both omnipotent and omniscient?

One reason why the incommensurability of values may not be a problem in theism is because in the concept of God one is conceiving of a reality that is unsurpassably great, and uniquely so. Thus, there is no worry about, say, comparing the goods of friendship and art. Even if the latter are incomparable, we may think that it would be great or greater for a being to exist who is able to create and sustain a cosmos in which there is friendship and art than one that cannot.

The notions of divine perfection and being worthy of worship have been interwoven historically. In the Abrahamic faiths, God is held to be worthy of worship and obedience due to God's being maximally excellent. God is thus not deemed worthy of worship because of sheer power, but because of goodness.

Let us explore these attributes further in the context of three objections.

Objection one: God's being worthy of worship is incompatible with human dignity. James Rachels (1996) develops this argument, contending that if God is worthy of worship, then God must be worthy of our obedience. By Rachels' lights, this profoundly conflicts with human dignity, which requires that persons never cede their autonomy to some other being. The demand to worship God conflicts with our inalienable requirement to be autonomous, free thinking, mature persons.

Reply: Deeming God to be worthy of worship does not at all compromise one's dignity or value, and it only compromises one's *autonomy* in a way that can be emancipatory and good. First, in agreement with Rachels, one would need one's free, autonomous reasoning to recognize a being (God or any other agent) as good. One has to exercise one's own autonomous judgment that God is good or perfect in order to believe that the worship of God is fitting. We could not distinguish between worshipping God and, say, worshipping money unless we were able to make reliable judgments about the nature of each. So, worship does not involve a willy-nilly abandonment of one's own reason, though it would involve recognizing another being who is wiser than oneself. Yet such recognition would seem to be no more problematic than recognizing that someone else, Socrates say, is wiser than oneself.

Also, Rachels does not seem to take note that worship involves delight, pleasure and awe. In the case of the divine this would involve worshipers taking delight, pleasure and awe in supreme goodness. Cultivating such awe in a divine, unsurpassably good being may be less a slavish submission to an all-powerful magistrate, than an awesome delight in that which is maximally and overwhelmingly good.

Consider a second objection, this one from the standpoint of feminism and gender.

Objection two: Pamela Sue Anderson has charged that conceiving of God as perfect involves a male projection: "Giving supreme perfection, and authority, to the ideal of reason ensures [that] the man has his ultimate gender ideal: the omni-perfect Father/God ... this patriarchal ideal ensures the dominant authority of men who remain blinded by their vision of perfection, unaware of the implications for the 'rationality' of their beliefs concerning women, as well as non-patriarchal men" (Anderson 2014: 12–13). Anderson links the Christian concept of God's perfection with a philosophy that deni grates those who would give a more central role to desire, *eros*, and passion (as opposed to reason), and that marginalizes women and non-heterosexuals. She contends that while theistic traditionalists may lay claim to impartiality, this claim is unconvincing. By her lights, conceptions of God in terms of ideals of power and knowledge are themselves gendered. In the following passage, she advances the problem of evil against an Anselmian concept of God:

> If God is omni-perfect, why has half of the human race been treated unequally? Whether we think of female fetuses being aborted precisely because they are female, not male, or think of any sex crime, the legacy of patriarchal rule over women and non-patriarchal men leaves a wake of inexplicable injustice. "Why do the innocent suffer" might be given a philosophical justification, but when it comes to females who suffer for no other reason than they are born female, any "rational" defense gives an additional reason for patriarchal man to justify his gratuitous violence against innocent women which, in light of human history, will always be out of proportion to the rest of humanity.[1] (Anderson 2014: 13)

Reply: I believe that recognizing God as maximally good or perfect allows the concept of God to be used to combat patriarchal domination. Given that patriarchal domination is evil, it is unfitting to think of God as reflecting or supporting such an evil. Given that the abuse of women and the vulnerable is equally wrong,

[1] Pamela Sue Anderson was a personal friend who, sadly, died in 2017. Although I disagree with her here I highly recommend her work.

God must ipso facto be thought of as condemning such harms.

Appreciating this point is important when it comes to the interpretation of sacred scripture. If you believe that some things are evil—such as genocide, the oppression of women, or punishments for homosexuality—and you believe that there is some scripture in which these evils are commanded or tolerated by God, then you need to believe either that the scripture is wrong, or that it needs to be interpreted without such attributions to God. So, for example, some homosexual Christians have claimed that the condemnations of homosexuality in the Bible are actually directed, not at mature, consenting single-sex couples, but at temple prostitution. Some Christians have likewise taken passages in which it appears that God commands the execution of innocent persons as records of what many followers of God believed to be divine revelation, but which need to be seen in a time-frame of progressive revelation, in which God becomes more and more evident over time.

As for perfection and the problem of evil, this will be our topic in Chapter 5. We need only note here that the Abrahamic faiths do not claim that the evil that exists is justified or is not really evil. These traditions all hold that that which is evil should not occur. Given that God is the Creator and sustainer of the cosmos, it is believed that, while God could annihilate the cosmos, God instead seeks to redeem both those who are evil and the victims of evil. But this in no way implies that, from the position of such traditions, whatever happens is good or justified.

Consider a final objection to divine perfection: If God is truly maximally excellent, does that not place the divine beyond the grasp of our concepts and language? After all, our concepts and language are geared to our very imperfect, non-divine world. Might there be some-thing inappropriate about even trying to describe God? There are two traditional responses to this question: the cataphatic and apophatic. According to the cataphatic tradition, God can be described with positive attributes (God is good, all-knowing, etc.). For those in the apophatic tradition God is principally to be conceived of as "other." The objection, then, is that any philosophy of divine attributes will exceed the capacity of language and concepts to explore the divine.

Reply: This third objection is important and offers a reminder that in philosophy one can overstep boundaries in terms of authority and power. We can see this, for example, in matters of race and justice today. It seems quite inappropriate for someone who is not African American to claim to know what it is like to be African American, even if their empathetic imagination is vibrant and informed. It is at this point, however, that one needs to appreciate the versatility of concepts and language. Our literal language may break down in describing the divine, but that does not leave us entirely bereft of resources in terms of using analogies and metaphors. If God is described as Father or Mother, this need not be taken literally as God does not have a gender. But such metaphors can express ways in which the God revealed in sacred scriptures is, for example, more maternal or paternal. One can attribute to God power, knowledge, goodness, and so on, without supposing that God's possession of such attributes is anthropomorphic. As for there being moral boundaries in ascribing knowledge, while it may be presumptuous for a person of privilege to claim to understand the lives of those who are not so privileged, the God of the Abrahamic traditions is understood—literally or by analogy—to be opposed to the unjust and to be an advocate of the dispossessed and oppressed.

Before moving on to the next divine attribute, it is worth noting the importance of God's otherness. Without a sense that God is profoundly different from creatures, we lose the idea that God could be worthy of worship, that God exists necessarily, and we can make the mistake of thinking that, if God exists, then God is some kind of super-human. This appears to be a mistake made by the biologist Richard Dawkins (2006), who describes the "God hypothesis" in terms of positing a being that is super-human. To be sure, some holy scripture uses anthropomorphic language to describe God— there are, for example, references to God's hands and eyes—but most see this as metaphorical. (Imagine a literal interpretation of the Biblical verse "the eyes of the Lord run around the world.")

Divine necessity

This element in the philosophy of God was encountered in Chapter 1. Many philosophers hold that, if God exists, God is not contingent, but exists necessarily in the sense that God could not not exist. Some philosophers have advanced an argument to the effect that if it is even possible that God exists necessarily, then God exists. This is often called the ontological argument. I develop a short version of the argument here, inspired by the medieval philosopher Anselm.

When it comes to necessary truths or necessary beings (if there are any), their truth and existence is not contingent: it cannot turn out that they merely happen to be true or to exist. To go back to our example from Chapter 1, it cannot just accidentally be true that $1 + 1 = 2$ or that it only is true on Mondays. The claim is either necessary or impossible. If a proposition is possible then it may or may not be necessary, but it is not impossible. Here is a succinct version of the ontological argument:

1. If God exists, God exists necessarily.
2. God's existence is either necessary or impossible.
3. If God's existence is possible, God's existence is not impossible.

4. If God's existence is not impossible, then God exists necessarily.
5. If God exists necessarily, then God exists.

The first two premises seem reasonable. The third is more controversial, but it may be supported by a principle that can be used in arguing that some state of affairs is possible:

If some state of affairs can be conceived of as existing (or pictured or imagined or described as existing), and one knows of nothing that makes such a state of affairs impossible, then one has some reason to believe that the state of affairs is possible.

I have defended a principle of this form in several places. It is fairly modest since it does not claim to prove that something is possible, only to formulate the conditions under which one would have some reason to believe that something is possible.

Some philosophers claim that it is not possible that God exists. This will be addressed in our discussion of the next divine attribute, God's being incorporeal or non-physical. But if the arguments for God's impossibility can be met, one would have some reason to believe that God's existence is possible and therefore necessary.

I raise this argument here for your further reflection, rather than seeking to develop it at length, but I will offer two quick objections and replies.

Objection one: The argument simply defines God into existence. You could imagine that there is a perfect, necessarily existing unicorn, and if that seems possible to you, you would then have an argument that such a unicorn exists.

Reply: The concept of a unicorn is simply the concept of a contingent thing, whereas the concept of God uniquely refers to a being whose very nature includes existence. If we upgrade the concept of a unicorn to include all the divine properties (omniscient, omnipresent, omnipotent, incorporeal, and so on), then we will be using the term "unicorn" as a kind of metaphor for God.

Objection two: The argument treats God's existing necessarily as a property. But existence itself is not a property and not part of any concept. To start an argument with the concept of an actually existing unicorn is akin to starting an argument with the concept of an actually existing God.

Reply: The concepts of existing necessarily, and related concepts such as existing contingently and being impossible, are all bona fide concepts and properties. The existence of unicorns is properly considered a contingent state of affairs. The existence of a square circle is an impossible state of affairs. And 1 + 1 = 2 is a necessary state of affairs. (See Yujin Nagasawa 2017 for discussion of this and other objections.)

Incorporeality

Some philosophers have problematized conceptions of God as incorporeal, immaterial or non-physical on the grounds that the only awareness we have of persons or agents is as embodied, material beings. We know what it is like to think about and address each other in the material world, but what about a being that is in some sense disembodied?

There are at least two points to consider in reply. First, it might be questioned whether we do have a clear concept of what it is to be physical or material. In Chapter 1 it was proposed that we have a clearer understanding of the mental than we do of a mind-independent physical world. We can go further here by taking note of how contemporary science seems to undermine the notion that we have a problem-free concept of the physical. The entry on materialism in the prestigious *Oxford Companion to Philosophy* captures this new, less-settled understanding of the concept:

Photons and neutrons have little or no mass, and neither do fields, while particles pop out of the void, destroy each other, and pop back in again. All this, however, has had remarkably little overt effect on the various philosophical views that can be dubbed "materialism", though one might think it shows at least that materialism is not the simple no-nonsense, tough-minded alternative it might once have seemed to be. (Honderich 1995: 530)

In keeping with this view, some philosophers contend that, whatever turns out to be physical, it is difficult to directly identify conscious, experiential states in the physical world. Colin McGinn, for instance, writes of the apparent disparity between consciousness and physical things and processes:

The property of consciousness itself (or specific conscious states) is not an observable or perceptible property of the brain. You can stare into a living conscious brain, your own or someone else's, and see there a wide variety of instantiated properties—its shape, colour, texture, etc.—but you will not thereby see what the subject is experiencing, the conscious state itself. (McGinn 1991: 10–11)

Likewise, Michael Lockwood, though himself a materialist, acknowledges that "the very existence of consciousness seems to me to be a standing demonstration of the explanatory limitations of contemporary physical science" (Lockwood 2003: 447). I therefore simply note here that some leading philosophers question the adequacy of materialism.

Second, consider the claim that our mental lives are not numerically identical to our physical bodies. This is sometimes called the *knowledge argument*, which will be developed below in three stages. While the argument is often used to support *dualism*, I present it here in support of *pluralism*: the view that rather than there being only one kind of thing (the physical), or two, there are many kinds of things (at least, there is more than the physical).

Stage one involves a principle of identity: If what appear to be two things are actually the same thing, then whatever is true of one, is true of the other. So, Sam Clemens and Mark Twain are two names for the same person. If Sam Clemens is indeed Mark Twain then whatever is true of Sam Clemens is true of Mark Twain. To shake hands with Twain is to shake hands with Clemens.

Stage two: If your mental states (thoughts, feelings, emotions, etc.) are the very same thing as your bodily states, then whatever is true of one is true of the other.

Stage three: Whatever is true of your mental states is not true of your body or bodily states. You can know all about a person's anatomy, brain states and all, but that alone will not give you knowledge of the person's thoughts, feelings, and so on. You may infer what a subject is thinking from observing their brain states, but that does not count as directly knowing what the subject is thinking.

If this argument holds up, then we have reason for believing that there is more to us than our bodily life. Versions of this argument can be found in the works of a number of philosophers, from Goethe and Bertrand Russell to Thomas Nagel, who famously wrote a paper entitled "What is it like to be a bat?" in which he argues for the distinctness of the mental and the physical on the grounds that you can have an exhaustive understanding of a bat's physical states but still have no idea about the bat's mental life.

Consider two objections:

Objection one: The argument only establishes that our concepts of the brain and of thinking are different, not that the brain and thinking themselves actually are different.

Reply: This seems too weak a conclusion. When we are aware of our thoughts and feelings we are aware of an activity or a state, not just the concept of an activity or a state. Likewise, when observing a person's (or a bat's) physical body and processes we are not observing concepts but things and events.

Objection two: If the mental and physical are distinct, what then accounts for their interaction? Isn't it anti-scientific to distinguish the mental and physical?

Reply: This is too big an objection to address in detail here, but I would suggest that the interaction between our mental life and our bodily life is the most well-observed, recognized fact about us. That a brain injury can cause us to lose consciousness, and that our thinking, emotions, and feelings define our lives (consciously and sub-consciously), seem indisput-able. The fact that scientists cannot directly observe the mental states and experiences of persons has not prevented fruitful scientific work in neurology and all those branches of science that address human and animal life.

Omnipotence

It is central to most concepts of God or gods that they are powerful. In the Abrahamic faiths, God is believed to exercise power in creating and conserving the cosmos and, indeed, is deemed almighty or omnipotent. This should not be interpreted as suggesting that God alone has power. If God creates beings that have causal powers themselves, including the power to act freely, this would involve God's creating beings that God does not meticu-lously and exclusively control. One might interpret such a creation as a matter of God limiting divine omnipo-tence, but it may just as well be seen as an expression of God's power. God is so powerful that God can create and sustain creatures who have freedom and are able to think, feel, and act in ways that are not prescribed or fully determined by God.

Omnipotence is best understood as a divine attribute—that is, as a property of God—rather than conceived of abstractly in relation to any subject whatsoever. If we take up the analysis of omnipotence abstractly then we run into a host of logical puzzles. Some of these can be handled by claiming that an all-powerful being is not limited just because it cannot bring about logically impossible states of affairs. If it is a fact that no being, not even God, can make a square circle in two-dimensional space (a figure that simultaneously has and does not have four right angles), this should not be seen as a limitation at all, since it is impossible for there to be a square circle. Some puzzles are similarly a matter of impossible things. Consider this famous paradox:

If God is omnipotent, God can create a stone so heavy that no one can lift it.
If God is omnipotent, God can lift any stone.
Therefore, God is not omnipotent for either God cannot create a stone so heavy that no one can lift or God cannot lift any stone.

The paradox dissolves once we see that the following state of affairs is as impossible as a square circle: there is a stone so heavy that it cannot be lifted by a being that can lift any stone. If we didn't dismiss such paradoxes as logically incoherent, then we would be left with a virtually infinite number of absurd things that an omnipotent being cannot do: eat porridge that cannot be eaten, grow a tree that cannot be grown, climb a mountain that cannot be climbed, and so on ad infinitum.

Another reason for locating our understanding of omnipotence in the context of the philosophy of God is to make clear that, in the Abrahamic faiths, it is the goodness or perfection of God that is key, not power per se. The power attributed to God is therefore not sheer or bare power, but the power befitting a being of maximal excellence. So, many (but not all) theists believe that certain powers are not divine or perfect, such as the power to lie, to do evil for the sake of evil, and all sorts of wicked acts. This is not, however, a limitation on a perfect being but a reflection of the nature of perfection itself.

Omniscience

Most philosophical work on the attribute of omniscience concerns its scope. The most vexing issue is whether omniscience of future free action is compatible with such action being truly free. Intuitively, it seems that a person acts freely only if they could have acted differently. If God (or anyone) knows with certainty that you will freely donate money to Oxfam tomorrow, can you do otherwise? The question arises not from the standpoint of the knower controlling what you do, but only of their knowing what you will do with certainty. So, if God knows now what you will do tomorrow, can your future action truly be free, that is, can it still be up to you to change your mind and act differently from what God knows you will do?

One response to this perplexity is to deny that future free acts can be known with certainty in advance. In philosophy of religion this view is expressed in what is called *open theism*. Those who adopt this position sometimes argue that for something to be true, there must be something that grounds this truth. It is the fact that Donald Trump is the President of the United States in 2018 that grounds the truth of the claim that he is the current US President. Some open theists argue that, in the case of future free action, since the action has not yet taken place, it is neither true nor false today that tomorrow you will, for example, freely give to Oxfam. Once you freely do so, this can be known, but not until then. This position is sometimes bolstered by a theory of time called *presentism*: the view that only the present is real. This is not the same as holding that the past and future are illusions—there are truths about the past — but it does stress the reality of what is occurring now. The past is real, but it is no longer present.

Open theism has its able defenders today, but there are also some philosophers who are unimpressed by the paradox of knowing future free action. They reason that if our knowledge of past free action does not prevent such action from being free, why should our knowledge of future free action? As for the grounding problem, some philosophers adopt what is often called four-dimensionalism, according to which all moments of time are equally real. This is sometimes accompanied by the view that God transcends time: God is not in time at all; what for us is future may be evident to God from a timeless vantage point.

Let us then move on to the philosophy of God and time.

Eternal or everlasting

While open theists understand God to be in time, and thus believe that when you pray to God now, God is hearing and responding to your prayer now, most theists, historically and today, think that God is outside of time. Those who think the latter often refer to God as eternal, whereas those who believe God to be temporal refer to God as being everlasting (in time, but without temporal beginning or end). One motive for thinking God eternal is cosmological: some theists believe that God created time. Another has to do with God's perfection. It has been argued that to be in time is to have an identity that is, as it were, spread out in time. A fuller, more appropriate view is that God has a fullness of being that transcends the moment. Consider this early statement of God's eternity by St. Augustine:

Nor dost Thou by time, precede time: else shouldest Thou not precede all times. But Thou precedest all things past, by the sublimity of an ever-present eternity; and surpassest all future because they are future, and when they come, they shall be past; but Thou art the Same, and Thy years fail not. Thy years neither come nor go; whereas ours both come and go, that they all may come. Thy years stand together, because they do stand; nor are departing thrust out by coming years, for they pass not away; but ours shall all be, when they shall no more be. Thy years are one day; and Thy day is not daily, but Today, seeing Thy To-day gives not place unto tomorrow, for neither doth it replace yesterday. Thy To-day, is Eternity; therefore didst Thou beget The Coeternal, to whom Thou saidst, This day have I begotten Thee. Thou hast made all things; and before all times Thou art: neither in any time was time not. (Augustine 1997: Book 11)

And here is a famous passage about God's eternity from Boethius:

God is eternal; in this judgment all rational beings agree. Let us, then, consider what eternity is. For this word carries with it a revelation alike of the Divine nature and of the Divine knowledge. Now, eternity is the possession of endless life whole and perfect at a single moment. What this is becomes more clear and manifest from a comparison with things temporal. ...

For it is one thing for existence to be endlessly prolonged, which was what Plato ascribed to the world, another for the whole of an endless life to be embraced in the present, which is manifestly a property peculiar to the Divine mind. (Boethius 1897, V.VI.)

Both views of God—as in time or as atemporal—will lead to different views of divine love. According to the view that God is outside of time, God is not subject to temporal passage (there is no before, during, and after for God), and thus, in a sense, God is changeless (or immutable). This may seem altogether at odds with Biblical portraits of God's love and activity. Traditionalists explain such changes to God (God is first revealed to Abraham then to Moses) on the grounds that God timelessly wills these changes. On this view, God timelessly wills that there be creation, revelation, incarnation, and so on, and God's love may be understood as timelessly directed towards all persons and creatures, in all galaxies and dimensions of reality, in what for us is the past, present, and future. From the perspective of open theism, however, the acts and love of God and creatures take place in the existential present moment. Because open theists insist on an undetermined future, many of them describe both God and creatures as facing an unknown future with real risks. William James offers this classic portrait:

> Suppose that the world's author [God] put the case to you before creation, saying "I am going to make a world not certain to be saved, a world the perfection of which shall be conditional merely, the condition being that each several agent does its own 'level best.' I offer you the chance of taking part in such a world. Its safety, you see, is unwarranted. It is a real adventure, with real danger, yet it may win through. It is a social scheme of co-operative work genuinely to be done. Will you join the procession? Will you trust yourself and trust the other agents enough to take the risk?" (James 2000: 127)

I leave it to the reader to explore these alternative views of God and time. I find much to admire in each. I am drawn to open theism's existential stress on the present moment. On the other hand, the idea of the fullness of divine life in the portrait of God's timeless eternity seems awesome, and puts a check on the way some of us are tempted to form anthropomorphic views of God. I have actually published defenses of both positions.

Alternative models of God and of what is real

While classical theism in the Abrahamic traditions dis-
tinguishes between God and the created order, there are
variations of theories which see the world as being in
some way a kind of body of God. This is sometimes
expressed by the term *panentheism*, meaning literally
everything ("pan") being in God. For many classical
theists, one compelling reason not to think of the cosmos
as in some way contained in God is that the cosmos is
contingent, while God exists necessarily. Panentheists,
however, will sometimes distinguish between aspects of
the divine such as God's necessary existence and the
created order understood as a kind of contingent extension of Godself. Most panentheists recognize the reality
of freedom in creatures—so that created persons are not
like parts of our bodies which are largely controlled by
us as agents—but they understand the way we treat
ourselves and the natural world in relation to God as
being profoundly proximate. To harm other people or
the natural world is likened to harming the divine, not
unlike the way in which if your arm is harmed, you are
harmed. This strong identity of God and the world has
been invoked recently by Sallie McFague to argue that
there are compelling religious reasons to care for the
planet in terms of climate change and global warming.

There are even more radical views of the divine that
deny any real (metaphysical) difference between the
world and the divine. This is an element in monistic
forms of Hinduism. We took note in Chapter 3 of the
monism of Shankara, affirming the unitary, sole reality
of Brahman. Consider this more extended portrait of
how our experience of the world of differentiated, individual objects is the result of illusion:

Brahman is neither the gross nor the subtle universe.
The apparent world is caused by our imagination, in its

ignorance. It is not real. It is like seeing the snake in the
rope. It is like a passing dream—that is how a man
should practice spiritual discrimination, and free himself
from his consciousness of this objective world. Then let
him meditate upon the Identity of Brahman and Atman,
and so realize the truth. ...

Give up the false notion that the Atman is this body,
this phantom. Meditate upon the truth that the Atman
is "neither gross nor subtle, neither short nor tall", that
it is self-existent, free as the sky, beyond the grasp of
thought. Purify the heart until you know that "I am
Brahman". Realize your own Atman, the pure and
infinite consciousness. Just as a clay jar or vessel is
understood to be nothing but clay, so this whole
universe, born of Brahman, essentially Brahman, is
Brahman only—for there is nothing else but Brahman,
nothing beyond That. That is the reality. That is our
Atman. Therefore, "That art Thou"—pure, blissful,
supreme Brahman, the one without a second. (Shankara
1970: 73–4)

At the end of the next chapter I offer an argument for
the plausibility of this concept of the divine.

Summary

In this chapter we have surveyed the philosophy of
divine attributes, considered the ontological argument
for theism, and observed the importance of non-theistic
concepts of the divine. The divine attributes have important roles in the Abrahamic faiths. For example, the idea
that God or Allah is everywhere present is articulated
in terms of God's power and knowledge. To say that
God is here, for example, is to claim that what exists
here is created and conserved in existence by God, that
God knows its properties and can exercise power in this
place. In terms of the incarnation, Christians take different views. As most Christians believe God is triune

they propose that, while there is one God, within the Godhead there are three persons, Father, Son, and Holy Spirit. Some claim that when the Son became incarnate as Jesus of Nazareth, he limited or gave up the divine attributes of omnipotence, omniscience, and omnipresence. The Son cannot give up the attribute of existing necessarily, but by becoming embodied the Son becomes subject to the contingencies of hunger, pain, death, and so on. Death could not bring about the annihilation of the necessarily existing Son, but it still involved a very real, painful death as the embodied Jesus of Nazareth. Other Christian philosophers accept what is called the two-minds account of the incarnation. On this model, God the Son retains all the divine attributes as a non-incarnate member of the trinity, but the incarnate Son's mind is limited to a mind within the overall mind, the way someone might maintain an overall vantage point as (for example) a playwright, but then enter the play as an actor. This is a profoundly limited analogy since the traditional belief in the incarnation is not a belief in someone play-acting. But insofar as the acting is taken to be real and robust the analogy may be useful.

Discussion questions

Omnipotence is traditionally understood as the power of a perfect, essentially good God. But would the power of such a perfect God be less than the power of another being (call it Molich) if that being had the power to do either good or evil? If the God of the Abrahamic traditions cannot lie, wouldn't this God be less powerful than Molich, who might be an all-powerful liar?

Is temporality—there being temporal change, or a before, during and after—essential for there to be thinking? It seems so, at least in our case. One cannot think, let alone speak, without taking some period of time to do so. One cannot think in an instant, for example, if by "instant" one means some non-durational point in time. If that is the case, and if God is beyond time/temporal change, does it follow that God cannot think?

Can the ontological argument be reversed? If it seems possible that God does not exist, wouldn't it follow that God's existence is not necessary? If God's existence is not necessary, then God's existence would be impossible.

4

Faith and Evidence

What is religious faith? There may not be a single answer to this question. Many philosophers have treated "faith" as requiring the holding of one or more beliefs that are true or false (whether or not we know them to be true or false). So, to have faith in the Christian tradition, for example, will involve a belief that there is a God, and so on. But belief alone seems not to be enough in order to understand the nature of religious faith; presumably some kind of trust also needs to be involved. Moreover, it would seem odd for a Christian to claim that she trusts her beliefs (even though she does), rather than the object of those beliefs. Some philosophers have proposed that "faith" might be more like having a generally positive attitude towards something, rather than directly believing that something is the case. One might have religious faith insofar as one has an allegiance or loyalty or hope, or feels as though one belongs in or to a religion.

All these suggestions are worthy of pursuit, but in this chapter the focus will be on religious beliefs about reality and the evidence for such beliefs, independent of matters of trust, positive attitudes, hope, loyalty, allegiance, and so on. Still, it is vital to recognize that the religious life is not only a matter of beliefs about what is real, and it is plausible to think that one might well practice a religion—by praying, for example— while only hoping rather than believing that a religion is true.

I first offer some general observations on the nature of evidence in philosophy of religion, and then turn to four arguments for theism: a cosmological argument different from that developed in Chapter 1; a teleological argument; a moral argument; and an argument from religious experience. I then develop an argument for Hindu monism and present a modest case for a Buddhist concept of the self.

Evidence about evidence

Evidence consists of the grounds that justify belief. In the case of philosophy of religion, some philosophers claim that the existence, order, and valuable nature of the cosmos counts as evidence for theism, while others claim that the vast occurrence of unjust suffering counts as evidence for its falsehood. Is it essential for a person to have evidence for their beliefs, whether religious or secular, in order for them to be justified? In this chapter, I shall be assuming that evidence is desirable, but let us pause to consider whether it is essential for justification.

The view that evidence is indeed essential for justified beliefs is sometimes called *evidentialism*. On a strong version of this position, a person is only justified in believing X if she is aware of evidence that justifies her belief. This seems fairly demanding. Many of us know things (or are not unjustified in our beliefs) in the course of our upbringing, daily living, and participation in society, without having an explicit awareness of the evidence for each of our beliefs. We might also have ordinary, justified beliefs in terms of what we perceive and observe and learn from others without being able to offer a defense of these beliefs in terms of evidence we may articulate on command. There are many demands on our time in terms of survival, work, raising families, and so on, such that evidentialism looks like a code for persons of leisure. Evidentialists in the history of ideas have also had a hard time specifying what exactly counts as sufficient evidence for our various beliefs. In courts of law and in managing special tasks (e.g., food safety, transportation, handling deadly chemicals, etc.) we have arrived at ways to distinguish responsible from negligent or reckless beliefs (and actions), but philosophers have backed away from earlier efforts to allow only infallible (incapable of error), incorrigible (not subject to correction) beliefs (as found in the seventeenth-century work of Descartes). In the world of philosophy today, positions are rarely advanced in terms of proofs. They are instead said to be backed up (or not) by good arguments or reasons, though it is rare to see claims that, in order to count as good, an argument must convince all fair-minded, well-informed inquirers. In darker moments, I sympathize with a colleague's "well" criterion for good arguments: he has produced a good argument for a position if he can get a few colleagues to say "well, you might be right."

There are two recent movements in philosophy of religion that have sought to bolster a non-evidentialist methodology.

According to reformed epistemology, a person may be justified in their Christian belief if that belief has been brought about by a reliable means, whether or not the person is aware of any evidence for their belief. Let's say Miriam simply forms the belief that God loves the world. If a loving God exists and Miriam's belief is formed through a reliable means, then she is justified (or warranted) in her belief. The reliable means may be an inchoate sense of the divine (*sensum divinitas*), or perhaps just the following of a reliable tradition. There is a view called *reliabilism* that offers some support for this position, treating justification as an external matter (the reliable means of producing beliefs) as opposed to an internal one (that stresses the subjective measuring of evidence by persons).

This is an interesting position. In my view, it may be correct, but it would not help those of us who have not had the *sensum divinitas* or have doubts about the overall framework of Christian theism. In other words, a skeptic may concede that if there is a God who directs you to reliably recognize God's reality, then you would be warranted in such a belief, but this outcome would do little to persuade the skeptic that you are so warranted.

A second movement in relation to evidence has been defended by Paul Moser, a Christian philosopher who contends that an all-good God would not prize knowledge of God that did not involve a moral transformation of the inquirer. Moser maintains that a mere spectator's awareness of God might be a matter of vanity or curiosity, whereas a morally perfect God would instead only become evident to persons who commit themselves to be morally and spiritually transformed by God. Moser proposes that if persons seek to follow the God of Christian scripture they will develop a transforming love of God and others (including their enemies) so radically that their transformed lives will become evidence, at least for the believer, that the Christian faith is true.

This position is not easy to assess. Of course, at least in principle, lives may be changed positively by worldviews that are not true, whether they be religious or secular. Also, to return to a point made in the introduction, without there being some evidence for a religious worldview available to the uninitiated, it is hard to see why someone might convert to that view and seek to cultivate its virtues.

While both reformed epistemology and Moser's position are bold, interesting proposals, in this chapter we will focus on some of the classical ostensible evidence for theism, before going on to look at a philosophical case for two non-theistic religious worldviews.

Four theistic arguments

Cosmological arguments

We considered a version of the cosmological argument in Chapter 1. Let us now address a second version: the Kalam argument (so called because the argument has roots in Muslim philosophy; "Kalam" is Arabic for "word" or "speech," as in Kalam Allah, meaning word of God). Why do you and I exist? Clearly, we are contingent and dependent on the causal powers of other things and conditions. There are three promising explanations: 1) We depend on other things, which depend on other things, which depend on still other things and so on to infinity. 2) We depend on other things that, some 13.5 or more billion years ago, originated from nothing. Or 3) Among all the causes of our being, there exists a being without a beginning that is not dependent on other causes. To defenders of the Kalam argument, this latter explanation, invoking the God of classical theism, allows us to avoid both an infinite regress and the claim that something comes from nothing.

While it may seem that some scientists today are prepared to entertain the second option, this turns out to not be the case. For example, some physicists contend that the cosmos emerged from fluctuating quantum energy. But this is not nothing, and thus not a violation of the precept that *nothing comes from nothing*. The first option might seem the most promising, but (as argued by William Craig, one of the foremost defenders of the Kalam argument) the positing of actual infinites leads to seemingly preposterous (or at least counter-intuitive) results. A quick clarification: there is an important difference between what is called an actual infinite and a potential infinite. The latter is a series that may be indefinitely extended, like a person counting 1, 2, 3, etc., forever—a process that will never be completed because there is no greatest possible number. An actual infinite is a series that is extant; for example, all whole numbers. Consider a thought experiment that brings to light the paradoxical nature of there being actual infinites. Imagine you are managing a hotel with infinitely many rooms. Each of the rooms is full and the guests are all paying $100. Imagine that the guests in every thousandth room leave. How many people have checked out? Infinitely many. How much less income do you have? You are losing out on infinite dollars. But is your income any less? No, you are still getting infinitely many dollars. Now imagine every room whose number is divisible by 3 is vacated. Same questions. In this case, too, you would have infinitely less income, but still just as much income. There are many other, similar thought experiments in the literature but most of them have the same structure, e.g. a library with infinitely many books which has infinitely many books withdrawn but no less books. Craig and others contend that the concept of an actual infinite has a role to play in some mathematical systems, but that there are no actual infinites in reality. By analogy, there are no philosophical obstacles to recognizing negative integers in mathematics, but it is another thing to posit negative things and facts in reality.

It might be thought that, if God is infinite, then the case against the existence of an actual infinite would be a case against the existence of God. But infinity is rarely advanced as a divine attribute, and, if God is timeless, God has not existed for an actual infinity of time. Also, some of the attributes discussed in the last chapter are related to potential but not actual infinites. If God is omnipotent, God can bring about any state of affairs compatible with the other divine attributes, but that would not entail that God can do infinitely many things.

As with the arguments that follow, my goal here is only to satisfy the "well" criterion noted above, or perhaps an even weaker version: "well, that is interesting and worthy of further thought"!

Teleological arguments

We not only live in a contingent cosmos and causally depend on other things and events, but our cosmos appears to be constituted by stable powers and forces, with laws of nature that allow for (or have generated) planets, stars, and galaxies, which (at least on our planet) have brought forth life, including animal life in which subjects have thoughts, experiences, agency, emotions, at least the appearance of freedom, an awareness of good and evil, and moral and religious values. Some teleological arguments take the form of an appeal to how the conditions for the emergence of our cosmos are so fine-tuned (if the force of gravity were different, there may not have been any stars or planets whatever) that this counts as evidence of a purposive, good Creator. Other versions of the argument take the form of weighing the evidence for or against theism or naturalism— which for our purposes we may treat as simply the denial of theism and the affirmation of nature—on the basis of the existence of our ostensibly good cosmos. It has been argued that, given theism, we have some reason for thinking that there would be a good cosmos, whereas, if naturalism is true, then there is no such reason.

There are, of course, multiple objections and replies. An appeal to Darwinian evolution may suffice to account for the diversity of life, without the need to posit a Creator who brings into being distinct species, but it would not account for the laws of physics and chemistry that make any biological life possible.

One recent reply to teleological arguments is to claim that our universe is one of many (perhaps infinitely many) universes. This is sometimes called the multiverse thesis. It is argued that, given infinitely many universes, it should not surprise us that ours exists, complete with life and its fine-tuned, ostensibly purposive structure. This is a fascinating and radical move, but it might be noted that there is no independent evidence of there being such universes; and even if there are infinitely many (or a great many) such universes, theism may still be better positioned than naturalism to explain them. Furthermore, there being infinitely many possible universes does not entail that all universes would be realized. There may be a possible universe in which a monkey types all the works of Shakespeare, but it also seems possible that this would never occur. Moreover, if the Kalam argument is plausible, there may be good reasons for doubting actual infinites.

Moral arguments

Some philosophers argue that the existence of objective moral facts—justice and compassion are good; cruelty and oppression are evil—is evidence of theism. They contend that biological evolution can give an account of what survives, but not of whether what survives is good or bad, right or wrong. Other philosophers have taken a different approach, conceding that the reality of objective morality is compatible with there not being a God, but that objective morality makes more sense and may be seen as more fitting in a theistic rather than naturalistic universe. This kind of reasoning has a long lineage going back to Plato in the fourth century BCE. While Plato contended that we should be good for goodness' sake, he also invoked a myth or narrative involving life beyond death in which the good are rewarded and tyrants are punished.

It is important to note that very few, if any, current moral arguments for theism involve claiming that atheists are not as well motivated to be good (or are in fact less good) than theists. Such arguments were popular in the early modern era, until the mid-nineteenth century, but since then moral arguments have focused on whether theism (or its alternatives) provide better accounts of what many of us assume to be the existence of real values and disvalues, good and evil.

An argument from religious experience

It was noted in Chapter 1 that some philosophers have contended that there can be experiential evidence of the divine. This is not empirical evidence *per se*, insofar as it is not the same as appealing to (for example) perceptions of the world around us, but it does involve appealing to a sense of God or the divine which is analogous to ordinary perception. In the following passage, Keith Yandell contends that the experience of the divine (which he refers to as *numinous experience*) is analogous to the perceptual experience of physical objects. Both involve what he characterizes as an act-object framework in which an activity (experiencing/perceiving) has an ostensible (apparent) object:

> If there is experiential evidence for any existential proposition, perceptual experiences provide evidence that there are physical objects; it is arbitrary not to add that perceptual experience provides evidence that God exists, unless there is some epistemically relevant difference between sensory and numinous experience. The crucial similarities are that both sorts of experience are "intentional" and have phenomenologies, or can be expressed via "intentional" phenomenological descriptions. That perceptual experiences have sensory fillings or phenomenologies, and numinous experiences do not, by itself seems no more reason to think that

> numinous experience in no way supports the proposition
> *There is a God* than does the fact that numinous
> experiences have theistic fillings or phenomenologies,
> and perceptual experiences do not, by itself provides
> reason for thinking that perceptual experience in no
> way supports the proposition *There are no physical
> objects.* (Yandell 1984: 28)

I suggest that this argument is best presented using an appearance principle, such as: *If something appears to be the case, then that is a reason for thinking it is the case, other things being equal.* The principle thus allow for defeaters: those realizations that discount the reliability of what appears to you. If it appears to you that you are seeing a huge butterfly then that would be a reason to believe what you are seeing, unless you realize that you have just taken some hallucinogenic or that the butterfly (as seen by you) is anatomically impossible (e.g., it passes through walls).

An argument from religious experience may take this structure:

> Premise one: If some state of affairs appears to a subject to be appearing to the subject then that is a reason, in the absence of defeaters, to believe that the appearing is reliable. This is a phenomenological claim, not merely the report of a subject's having a belief that some state of affairs exists. The difference would be between a person who thinks there is a God (for whatever reasons) and a person who believes that they are being appeared to by God.

> Premise two: Many people in many cultures appear to experience the divine: a transcendent, sacred, good or holy reality.

> Conclusion: If there is no reason to believe that such appearances are false, it is reasonable to believe that such perceptions are reliable.

The plausibility of this argument will depend, in part, on one's overall philosophy of the divine or God. If there are independent reasons for thinking that there is no divine reality, then reports of experiencing the divine are naturally going to be discounted. If, on the other hand, there are some good (though perhaps not compelling) reasons for thinking there is a divine reality, then such reports will gain in potential evidential significance. This appeal to the overall philosophical setting of our beliefs comes to the fore in the following objection by Bruce Russell:

> Suppose someone appears to me in my dreams who looks like my deceased grandmother and seems to be unselfishly loving and forgiving. Suppose she appears again and again, night after night, year after year. Suppose, further, that as a result of these dream experiences my life changes for the better, and I come to believe that my grandmother still exists in some way. Imagine that as a result of the experiences of my grandmother in my dreams I become a better person, more loving and forgiving, even of my enemies. Wouldn't the best explanation of those experiences be that they were somehow produced by me alone, say, by the neurons in my brain firing in certain ways, and wouldn't the best explanation of the change in my life be that *my belief* that my good and loving grandmother still exists and wants me to become more unselfishly loving somehow caused those changes? There is no need to posit the existence of my grandmother to explain either my experiences of her or the changes in my life. (Russell 2009)

Assessing this (amusing) objection would involve comparing religious narratives with the grandmother story. In religious narratives of experiences of the divine, they are often interwoven with communities of believers, with multiple accounts of multiple people coming to sense a holy, divine reality, which is rather different from a single person dreaming of his grandmother. (For a good defense of the argument from religious experience, see Kai-Man Kwan 2011; for a critique see Martin 1990.)

Developing the argument from experience as well as critiquing it will involve assessing the compatibility of different accounts of the divine or sacred. If John Hick's thesis (noted in Chapter 2) that different religions are different modes of accessing the same reality is correct, then diverse religious experiences will not turn out to challenge the authenticity of the religious experiences of others.

An argument for monism

As a partial source of evidence for monism, I will offer a line of reasoning to the effect that you and I are not strictly speaking identical with ourselves as distinct, non-identical things, but we are in some way modes of something bigger. The argument does not entail the existence of Brahman (world soul) and Atman (the individual soul), but it does direct us away from thinking that our identity as a distinct individual is what might be considered an ultimate fact. The argument rests on recognizing the possibility that you or I could have had very different lives. As I do not know all my readers, I will choose a friend in developing the line of reasoning.

First premise: I could have been Veronika.

This might be supported by an appearance principle (as introduced above). I know Veronika very well, and can picture, imagine, describe, and appreciate what it would be like to have been born in Munich, to have been parented by musicians, to be an Alpine climber. Some philosophers (especially materialists) believe that a person's origin could not have been different than it was; for example, you could not have had different parents or have developed from a different fertilized egg. Let's acknowledge here that this may be a serious objection, but, if we do not know that materialism is true, then the fact (if it is one) that you can imagine having a very different life would be some reason to think that this is a real possibility. This might be further supported by the fact that when we engage with certain literary works (autobiographies for example), or are extraordinarily empathetic (identifying with another person), we can vividly think of the world through the lens of a different life.

Second premise: Charles Taliaferro could not have been Veronika.

Arguably, this thing (I say, as I point to myself) was born in New York City in 1952, went to kindergarten at Mrs. T's schoolhouse, etc., etc. Charles could not have been born in Munich, and so on.

If we adopt both premises I think it follows that I am not strictly speaking or solely identical with Charles Taliaferro. To be sure, I am (as it were) living the life of Charles Taliaferro, but the "I" when I use it in the sentence "I could have been Veronika" refers to something more than Charles or Veronika.

In the next and final section of this chapter, I will explore briefly how we might further challenge our confidence in our unique, separable identities.

A buddhist no-self argument

Consider Shankara's claim about the self or ego:

> Just as the word "chariot" is but a mode of expression for axle wheels, chariot body, pole, and other constituent members, placed in a certain relation to each other, but when we come to examine the members one by one, we discover that in the absolute sense there is no chariot; and just as the word "house" is but a mode of expression for wood and other constituents of a house, surrounding space in a certain relation, but in the absolute sense

> there is no house ... in exactly the same way the words
> "living entity" and "ego" are but a mode of expression
> for the presence of the five attachment groups [the
> components making up a person], but when we come
> to examine the elements of being one by one, we discover
> that in the absolute sense there is no living entity there
> to form a basis for such figments as "I am" or "I"; in
> other words, that in the absolute sense there is only
> name and form. The insight of him who perceives this
> is called knowledge of the truth.

Why would anyone support this stance? You might
support it if you engage in a certain form of introspec-
tion wherein what you recognize about yourself are
parts: desires, visual fields, different tastes, smells,
sounds and other sensations, different acts of the will,
thoughts, emotions. These will all be understood as
things you undergo or feel, but how confident are you
that the "you" is some kind of unchanging substance
behind or supporting all these components? Might it not
become more plausible to think of yourself as an ever
changing process, a series of relations and events that
are linked by memory and convention, but not as a
fixed, changeless reference point? (For a defense of this
position, read more of Shankara's *Crest-Jewel of Discrimination* (1970). For a critique, see Lund 2005.)

There are many more arguments that may provide
evidence for Buddhism, Hinduism, and theistic positions. There are, for example, arguments from consciousness, arguments from sanctity (the lives of saints
and holy sages), and an argument from the beauty of
the Qur'an. And it may be noted that if evidentialism is
not authoritative in its claim that all and only beliefs
are justified if they are supported by evidence, then the
grounds for religious and secular beliefs and practices
might rest less on evidence than on a person's sense of
well-being, fulfillment, meditative and prayerful practices, and so on. Moreover, there may be types of evidence for positions that are personal ("such and such a

position makes sense to me") that are difficult to formulate in impersonal, academic terms.

Discussion questions

It has been argued that people can know something without knowing that they know it. If this is true, might you know that some religious or secular view of reality is true but not know that you know it?

If a person experiencing what seems like a numinous divine reality is evidence that there is such a numinous, divine reality, is a person experiencing the absence of a numinous divine reality evidence of the non reality of such a being?

The arguments in this chapter have appealed more to evidence than to the impact of religious beliefs on a believer's life. But what if being a theist or a Buddhist or a Hindu made you more fulfilled, or more highly motivated to reach some of your goals (from matters of marriage to making friends to living life with minimal anxiety, and so on)? Would or should these be factors in seeking to adopt a religious or a secular worldview?

5

Problems of Evil and Good

In this chapter, let us assume an ordinary understanding of ills and goods. So, murder, rape, torture, slavery, and economic oppression are all wrong and ugly. Birth defects, prolonged suffering that seems to serve no purpose, warfare, deaths due to drought, floods, diseases, and other natural or human-made disasters are also evil and ugly. Let us further assume as evil and ugly the vices of vanity, unmotivated and irrational rage, willful infidelity and betrayal, the manipulation of innocent persons for the sake of personal gain, malicious contempt for others, especially for the vulnerable, stealing, especially from the innocent, kidnapping, hypocrisy and moral weakness, sexism, racism, speciesism, ageism, and human rights violations that lead to massive refugee crises. Suffering involving or caused by mental illness is also ugly and evil. This is obviously a woefully incomplete list.

Among events and things that may be considered beautiful and good, let us assume that there are beautiful human and non-human animals, plants and minerals. In human life, the good and the beautiful would include our powers to act, to sense and feel, to have emotions, to have ideals and exercise memory and reason, to form positive relationships with other humans and animals and the natural environment. Let us further assume that friendship, love between persons, respectful sexual intimacy and romance, the well-being of families, and just communities are good and beautiful, as are acting with courage, compassion, and respect, and the pursuit of justice and human flourishing. Let us also assume that our capacity to work and to share the benefits of our work with others is good and beautiful. While the misuse of our capacity for freedom and for moral and aesthetic judgment may be evil and ugly, those capacities, when used rightly, are also good and beautiful.

Is the cosmos as we experience it—with all these and many other ills and goods—something that might be created and sustained by an all-good, all-powerful, all-knowing God?

In philosophy of religion there are several important distinctions in the literature on the problem evil poses for theism, beginning with the difference between a theodicy and a defense. A theodicy offers an account of why it is that God actually does create and sustain this cosmos. This often takes the form of what is called the greater good defense, in which it is argued that some of the great goods in the cosmos require or make likely the great ills, but all in all, it is better that the cosmos is created and sustained rather than not. The passage that follows, from Keith Ward, suggests that evil, death, and destruction may be essential for the great goods in our universe (as well as in universes like ours):

> In some possible universes, including this one, it could well be that some suffering is inevitable. Modern science helps us to see this. If humans have evolved in our universe from a primeval big bang, then that process of evolution necessarily involves suffering and destruction. Stars had to explode to form the heavier elements of

which life is composed. Millions of organisms had to die in order for human life to evolve on this planet. Even now, humans have to destroy plant or animal life in order to survive. The physical laws of this universe depend upon destruction, mutation, conflict, and, therefore, destruction and death, if intelligent persons are to evolve in it. If we understood the laws of nature fully, we would see that such destruction and the suffering conscious beings feel when involved in it are inevitable consequences of having a universe like this. (Ward 2008: 79–80)

An alternative theistic approach to evil is called a defense. In a defense, the goal is to argue that the evils in the cosmos might (for all we know) be allowed by God for good reasons. Philosophers presenting such a defense tend to advance logical possibilities, rather than arguments that we are in possession of justified beliefs about the good reasons that God has for allowing evil. The distinction between a theodicy and defense emerged in the philosophy of religion literature during a famous exchange. The philosopher J. L. Mackie advanced a logical problem of evil, to the effect that theism entails there should be no evil whatsoever. Alvin Plantinga responded with what has come to be called the free will defense. According to this, it is possible that God creates free beings whose right use of their freedom God cannot then determine. Arguably, it is good for there to be free creatures. If so, their misuse of their freedom may be the price to be paid for their having the good of freedom.

Defenses are sometimes linked to what is called skeptical theism. This may seem an odd term, but the view is that while we should not be skeptical about theism— it is after all a reasonable belief—we should not expect to have a clear idea about why there is so much evil in the cosmos. So, in both a theodicy and a defense, there may be an appeal to the positive good of creatures with free will living interdependently, morally responsible for each other's welfare, but the defender only advances this as a possibility while a theodicist argues that we may see it as a greater good. Both Richard Swinburne and John Hick—two of the most widely known advocates of theodicy—thus insist that God's bringing about the good of freedom would involve God bringing about a great good, notwithstanding the horrors that come from the misuse of freedom. In the following passage Swinburne replies to the objection that God could both make us free and prevent us from doing serious harm to each other:

> The less [God] allows men to bring about large scale horrors, the less the freedom and responsibility he gives to them. What in effect the objection is asking is that a God should make a toy-world, a world where things matter, but not very much; where we can choose and our choices can make a small difference but the real choices remain God's. For he simply would not allow us the choice of doing real harm, or through our negligence, allow real harm to occur. He would be like an over-protective parent who will not let his child out of his sight for a moment. (Swinburne 1991: 219–20)

In this chapter, I cannot hope to settle the problem of evil, but I will commend taking four factors into account: the implication of the theistic problem of evil for our conception of the good of humanity and the world; the flawed notion of a best possible world; the importance of distinguishing justification and redemption; and the importance of distinguishing what may be called the ethics of the Creator and the ethics of creatures.

1) If one honestly believes that it would be better if the cosmos did not exist, then this can lead to profoundly anti-humanistic values. There is today an antinatalist movement in parts of the West which holds that the continuation of humanity as a species is not good and which thus questions the good of reproduction.

While the apparent cruelty in the natural world chronicled by Charles Darwin horrified the sensibilities of some philosophers, twentieth-century and contemporary ecologists like Aldo Leopold have promoted the idea that it is good that natural ecosystems involve suffering and death. Holmes Rolston has written on the overall value of evolution, contending that for there to be a world without predation and suffering would involve an almost fairytale biology (Rolston 2003: 534). Theists might grant that God can create worlds with radically different laws of nature—and perhaps God has done so—but that does not belie affirming that our world is still good, even if it is not the best possible world.

2) It has been argued that a maximally great Creator would only create the best possible world. We can conceive of worlds far better than ours, and so the fact that our world is not the best possible is a reason to think there is no maximally great Creator. Some philosophers object, however, that the very concept of a best possible world is flawed. Arguably, the notion is like the concept of the highest number: there could not be one. For any number you can imagine, there will always be that number plus one. So, imagine any world with happy creatures, no matter how many. There can always be a better world, just by adding one more happy creature. So, even God cannot create the best possible world.

3) It is sometimes thought that the Abrahamic faiths seek to (or need to) hold that the evils of the cosmos are justified or good. This seems wrong. Most theistic philosophers hold that evil should not occur; it is never good for there to be rape, murder, and so on. The reality of evil goes against the very nature and will of God. What most maintain, however, is that even if, from a moral point of view, a limitlessly good God should annihilate all evil, it is compatible with God's goodness that God seeks to redeem evil-doers.

How the redemption of evil-doers may take place will be discussed in the next chapter, but for a snapshot distinction between justification and redemption consider two types of cases. Justificatory goods are those that justify some act that involves some harm, as when a painful medical procedure has to be performed to save a person's life (the latter would be a justificatory good). A redemptive good is a good that is worthy of pursuit but that does not justify an act of harm. Imagine a loving couple entering into a crisis because, in a weak moment, one of them (Chris) betrayed the other (Pat). Imagine that Chris confesses, repents, and asks for forgiveness. Pat would be completely justified in ending the relationship, but she reconciles with Chris so that, in the end, they enjoy a great good: the redemptive good of reconciliatory love. In this case there is a good, but it in no way makes the betrayal good. In the next chapter we will look further into the nature of forgiveness and reconciliation.

4) One can approach the problem of evil thinking that God is like any other agent (perhaps a bystander), and reason that any good subject who had the power and knowledge to prevent an evil would do so. But in philosophy of religion the question is about what kind of cosmos would be created and sustained by an all-good God. To assess the problem of evil we need to use our imaginations on a cosmic scale, exploring whether life as we know it is compatible with an overall conception of a good Creator and sustainer of the cosmos. (Parenthetically, it should be noted that if one believes that, overall, life itself is not worthy of being created and sustained by an all-good God, then that may invite a very negative view of life itself, viz. that life is not worthy of our approval or affirmation.) Consider two possible worlds, Alpha and Beta, the first of which affirms the compatibility of evil with a general theism, but without any

commitments to a possible afterlife or a divine incarnation, and so on. Do you believe the world described in the following paragraph is possible?

Alpha: There is an omnipotent, omniscient, unsurpassably excellent, all-good, necessarily existing being who has created and sustains a cosmos of at least one hundred billion galaxies in which there are (perhaps uncountably) many planets, at least one of which sustains life (there may or may not be many billions of others). All the elements of this cosmos, with their causal powers and liabilities, are dependent upon divine creation and conservation such that none of them would endure over time without God's causal powers. The cosmos appears to be governed by uniform, stable laws such as we discover through physics, chemistry, and biology. The vastness and grandeur of this cosmos merits our awe and delight as something sublime and of extraordinary beauty. On earth, chemical bonding led to the emergence of life and, through a long, complex evolutionary history, the emergence of plant and animal life. Amid the multitude of non-human animal life, some developed and are developing powers of movement and sentience. With some mammals there emerge persons (selves or subjects) who have powers of movement, a range of senses and feelings, memory, reason, the power to love or hate, fear and desire, and (eventually) powers to make moral judgments and to act in light of what seem to be right or wrong choices, virtues and vices. Some use these powers for the good and welfare of other persons and forms of life, and are beautiful, but some are profoundly ugly and wrong. In this cosmos, there are good and beautiful friends, families, adventures, creative acts, and there are evil and ugly enemies, hateful rulers, and soul-destroying acts such as rape, torture, murder, enslavement, and oppression. These evils are contrary to the will and nature of God, abhorrent to God's purpose in creation. While God commands people not to murder, and judges each murderer guilty of a heinous crime and sacrilege, God does not miraculously intervene to prevent every murder. God seeks to be revealed to and enter into relationship with created persons through experiences and events. Through prophets and sages God calls people from evil toward a good and fulfilling life. In this cosmos there is the good of a healthy created life, but there is also great suffering, and all living things eventually perish.

Some philosophers, including some theists, maintain that Alpha is implausible. There are at least four elements that some theists insist would need to be added to Alpha. Beta is the same world as Alpha but with the following additions: God actively works in the cosmos to redeem those who are evil; God seeks to heal those who are subject to horrendous evil; God suffers with those who suffer; and life does not end in death, for God seeks to redeem persons in a life after death. In a short book such as this, there is not the space to develop a fuller picture of Beta, in which each of these elements are added in detail, but a full engagement with the theistic problem of evil would invite such an account. Instead, and by way of introducing the themes of the next chapter, I will cite here a Jewish philosopher who underscored the vital importance for theism of the possibility of an afterlife:

[W]ithout this belief [in an afterlife], it is simply impossible to make sense of the world as the creation of an all-good, all-powerful God. Without the eventual vindication of the righteous in Paradise, there is no way to sustain the belief in a providential God who watches over His chosen people. If death means extinction, there is no way to make sense of the claim that he loves and cherishes all those who died in the concentration camps—suffering and death would ultimately triumph over each of those who perished. But if there is eternal life in a World to Come, then there is hope that the righteous will share in a divine life. Moreover, the divine

> attribute of justice demands that the righteous of Israel who met their death as innocent victims of the Nazis will reap an everlasting reward. Here then is an answer to the religious perplexities of the Holocaust. The promise of immortality offers a way of reconciling the belief in a loving and just God with the nightmare of the death camps. As we have seen, this hope sustained the Jewish people through centuries of suffering and martyrdom. Now that Jewry stands on the threshold of the twenty-first century, it must again serve as the fulcrum of religious beliefs. (Cohn-Sherbok 1990: 292–3)

Those religions without a theistic God or Creator do not face the problem of evil as it has been engaged in this chapter. Buddhist philosophers, for instance, have not sought to defend the reality of Brahman in light of suffering; quite the opposite. The problem of evil is one reason, among others, why some Buddhist philosophers have developed arguments against Hinduism. And there are philosophies of God that also do not face the problem of evil with the same intensity as classical theism. For example, some philosophers such as John Bishop and Brian Davies adopt a version of theism which rejects the idea that God is a person or person-like, while Peter Bertocci is a theist who denies that God is all-powerful. As in Plato's understanding of God, God creates only the good; evils are the result of factors that God cannot control. Some philosophers have understood God to be more like our concept of The Good (an abstract property) rather than a purposive agent.

Discussion questions

If there cannot be a best possible world, does it follow that there cannot be a worst possible world?

If you believe that it is bad (or even evil) for non-human animals to suffer, would you have some

obligation to seek to reduce such suffering, e.g. by polic-
ing the natural world?

Some theists appeal to the existence of freedom as
one of the grounds for expecting the world to contain
evil. Do you believe that freedom is a basic good (good
for its own sake), or is it only good if it is used to bring
about good states of affairs?

How might a person's view of the goods and evils
discussed in this chapter have an impact on their personal life?

6

Love and the Limits of the World

In this chapter, we will look at religious values in four sections. In the last chapter we considered what role might be played by evil in light of a possible afterlife. In section one of this chapter, we explore some religious conceptions of loving persons and how they might motivate a philosophy of life, death, and life after death. In section two, we consider whether there are philosophical reasons for thinking that life after life is possible or plausible. In section three, we look at the value and reasonability of specific religious claims about revelation, prayers, and miracles. In section four we examine the relationship between religious and secular values.

Love, life, and death

Why would anyone desire or look for life after this life? It is perhaps obvious why we would desire an afterlife for people who die young or whose lives from the beginning have been full of suffering and terror. For those who (for whatever reason) lead impoverished lives, it is not a mystery why one might hope that there is some realm of fulfillment beyond this life. In the last chapter it was suggested that the bare possibility of life after life might open up an arena of goods and the possibility of redemption that is lacking in this life.

Let's first consider those who are highly critical of people who yearn for life beyond death, keeping in mind that in section two we will confront the question of the philosophical possibility of there being such an afterlife. Obviously, if an afterlife were known to be impossible, then hoping for it would hardly be consoling. If we know that there can be no life after death, then presumably we must live courageously in light of the fact that death is final (though allowing that those who die may "live on" in memory and in the effects of their lives on the world).

While the desire for a life after this life can be motivated by a true love of others—for example, in the desire of loving parents that their child not be annihilated at death—could it be that many people maintain a hope in the afterlife for vain, selfish reasons? Perhaps more than one person thinks: I am the center of the universe. After all, how can the world possibly go on without me? And who is to say that the continuation of life beyond this life would be good or desirable? A famous British philosopher, Bernard Williams, proposed that the continuation of life beyond death would be boring. And worse than boring are some traditional religious conceptions of hell in which people face eternal torment. The French philosopher, Jean Paul Sartre, wrote a play entitled *No Exit* in which the afterlife is portrayed as a horrifying, suffocating enclosure peopled by characters who are each depraved and bitter in their own ways. One of them famously concludes: "Hell is other people."

Let's concede that the above positions reflect real possibilities—an afterlife might be boring or hellish—but let's also give the other side its due. If we imagine life continuing in repetitive commonplace acts (an eternal game of golf or a never-ending feast, and so on), the temptation to think it boring is likely, though not inevitable. Repeated everyday activities, whether walking one's dog or making love, might be fine for most of us forever. Still, the British novelist and lay philosopher, G. K. Chesterton, likens the cosmos as conceived by certain materialists to a prison, and notes that its bare expansion in time and space would not be good news:

> I have remarked that the materialist, like the madman, is in prison, the prison of one thought. These people seemed to think it singularly inspiring to keep on saying that the prison was very large. The size of this scientific universe gave one no novelty, no relief. The cosmos went on forever, but not in its wildest constellation could there be anything really interesting; anything, for instance, such as forgiveness or free will. The grandeur or infinity of the secret of its cosmos added nothing to it. It was like telling a prisoner in Reading [jail] that he would be glad to hear that the [jail] now covered half the county. The warden would have nothing to show the man except more and more long corridors of stone lit by ghastly lights and empty of all that is human. So these expanders of the universe had nothing to show us except more and more infinite corridors of space lit by ghastly suns and empty of all that is divine. (Chesterton 2006: 56–7)

In addition to noting that the mere extension of life is not ipso facto desirable, we might also recognize that the intensity of some things and events we value in this life rest on their being short-lived and having an (apparent) absolute ending. (The intensity of our experience as, respectively, author and reader might skyrocket if we supposed this was the last writing I would do and the last book you would read!) Even so, some philosophers (like Chesterton) propose that the goodness and value of persons is not something that can be exhausted over time, and because of this the annihilation of persons at death would be more a tragedy than a factor that should lead us to value persons more.

I was drawn to Chesterton's thesis upon the death of my parents in 2004 and 2010. They were both ninety-five years old. From a bodily point of view, they seemed to have exhausted the health and value of life. Organs failed, strength collapsed. But while the good of their bodily life came to an end (after a fulfilling life), would I say that the person my father or mother was (or is) was also exhausted? That would seem loveless on my part. A look at some imaginative literature on this topic might help advance what I am suggesting.

What if those you love were to live healthy lives as long as those recorded in the Hebrew and Christian Bible, in which Noah lives to 350, Enoch to 365 (and then may not have died but have been taken heavenward), and Melchizedek to at least 465 years (according to sacred scripture)? Or, going further, think of the three centaur-like creatures in Madeleine L'Engle's delightful *A Wrinkle in Time*: Mrs. Who, Mrs. Which, and Mrs. Whatsit. The latter is the youngest at only two billion years old. Do these three ladies show any sign of descending into tedium? Things seem pretty exciting in their universe, what with helping other creatures fight evil forces ("the large black shadow"), their participation in the rapturous, ecstatic praise of God, and the like. In L'Engle's imaginary world, praising God involves a wild, enthralling choreographed joy, something quite alien to the British philosopher Thomas Hobbes, who wrote (perhaps disparagingly) of paying compliments to God. To appeal to a different fairy tale involving long tedium-free lives, imagine those you love lived as long as Gandalf in *The Lord of the Rings*, who spent 2,019 years wandering Middle Earth (as many years as Saruman and Sauron). In Tolkien's legendarium, Gandalf lived a mere 9,000 years before entering Middle Earth, and at the end of the books he does not perish but travels to the Undying Lands. Throughout Tolkien's trilogy there is a recognition of the gift and cost of love when immortality is given up by elves; this happens in battle and in Arwen's bond with Aragorn. Elves can be killed, but in Tolkien's world they can live forever. So, when Arwen meets Aragorn, while she looks young she is 2,700 years old. She becomes mortal, however, when lovingly united with Aragorn.

These imaginary works, like the Biblical texts, offer a robust witness to the intrinsic good and value of persons living well beyond their "natural" time span. (As an aside, if matters were reversed, and Aragorn stood to gain elfish immortality by marrying Arwen, then, had he preferred they both die, I suggest that Arwen might want to rethink their relationship.) In short, the hope that those you love will not be annihilated at death need not be motivated by selfish, vain desires—it can well be motivated by an arduous love. Let's briefly consider a philosophy of love.

While today the term "love" may be used willy-nilly, there is a longstanding Platonic tradition that identifies three dimensions of love focused on goodness. First, there is beneficent love. To love beneficently is to love and desire the good of the beloved. In terms of loving oneself or another person, one naturally desires the fulfillment of the one loved—taking pleasure in their well-being, feeling sorrow over their ills. Second, there is unitive love, which involves a desire to be united with the beloved. In romantic love this might involve eros, whereas in non-erotic love it may involve only a desire to be in the presence of the beloved. The third dimension of love is emulatory love. This might be thought of as an element of beneficent love, but is distinguishable from it because of its important role in most healthy forms of love. Emulatory involves a love or desire for the beloved at her best. Let's say you love Gandalf but not the fact that he is a smoker. In emulatory love you desire him to give up his pipe smoking (unless it is infrequent and not harmful to self or others). Because goodness is central to it, this philosophy of love in three dimensions allows us to distinguish healthy self-love from narcissism, and the healthy love of others from obsession; both narcissism and obsession can involve a craving or lust that is not at all loving of the goodness of all involved.

If life after death is conceived of as a realm of fulfillment and redemption, and if one believes such a life is possible, then loving another person would naturally involve a desire for them to enjoy such a realm. Moreover, if one has some reason to believe that there is an all-powerful Creator-God who loves his creatures, then this would naturally lead one to believe that such a God would desire and effect the fulfillment of creatures beyond death.

The philosopher Philip Kitcher has charged that to desire that persons should not perish at death is to desire that persons not be human (Kitcher 2014: Chapter 4). It may be that for many people the very concept of a human person surviving beyond death would be incoherent, but this seems like a minority position given that the vast majority of people today believe in some form of afterlife (whether reincarnation or continuation in another realm). It might also be added, that, for some of us, being human is not essential to being a person: there can be persons who are not human, including non-human animals, non-human persons on other planets, etc. Speaking personally, I would not object to being transformed at death into a Mr. or Mrs. or non-gender-specific griffin along the lines of L'Engle's beings. Moreover, some religions posit an afterlife for some non-human animals; in which case, to conceive of your dog Rudy will not ipso facto be to conceive of an animal, or the soul of an animal, that perishes at death. Rudy might live on.

(For those desiring a portrait of perpetual life not involving imaginary creatures, consider the Tarritopsis nutricula, a small creature related to the jellyfish which

has evolved to develop what is called transdifferentia-
tion, in which it can undergo a complete regeneration
of its entire body such that after reaching maturity it
can return to its juvenile polyp stage. This is an actual
creature that is believed to be capable of perpetual,
endless renewal. Of course, this would not impress
Bernard Williams, who rightly notes that humans have
powers, needs, and liabilities far different from jellyfish,
but it is an interesting case of what seems like elvish
immortality in our world.)

Perhaps the main reason why many religions do not
subscribe to Williams' idea that a life beyond this one
would be tedious is because they regard life itself as a
great gift. That we are alive at all is not necessary, but
contingent. Perhaps one tires of life when one takes it
for granted, assuming that to be alive at all is a run-of-
the-mill, prosaic certainty, merely the background to
what is truly interesting rather than a shockingly wild,
precious contingency. Chesterton urges us to recover the
startling surprise of being alive in his meditation on
Defoe's classic *Robinson Crusoe*:

> I have said that stories of magic alone can express
> my sense that life is not only a pleasure but a kind of
> eccentric privilege. I may express this ... feeling ... by
> allusion to [a] book always read in boyhood, *Robinson
> Crusoe* ... which owes its eternal vivacity to the fact
> that it celebrates the poetry of limits, nay, even the wild
> romance of prudence. Crusoe is a man on a small rock
> with a few comforts just snatched from the sea: the
> best thing in the book is simply the list of things saved
> from the wreck. The greatest of poems is an inventory.
> Every kitchen tool becomes ideal because Crusoe might
> have dropped it in the sea. It is a good exercise, in
> empty or ugly hours of the day, to look at anything,
> the coal scuttle or the bookcase, and think how happy
> one could be to have brought it out of the sinking
> ship on to the solitary island. But it is a better exercise
> still to remember how all things have this hairbreadth

escape: everything has been saved from a wreck. (Chesterton 2006: 58–9)

I leave it to you to decide whether you side more with Chesterton, Williams, or some other alternative.

So far, we have been contemplating a (perhaps wildly) optimistic conception of life after life. But what about the traditional conception of hell we find in some forms of Christianity and Islam, as well as in some versions of Judaism, Hinduism, Buddhism, Jainism, Sikhism and other traditions? There are multiple portraits of what might be covered by the term "hell." Perhaps what most people object to about the concept is that, in positing a realm of eternal punishment, it appears to be driven by base desires like resentment and the desire for revenge. One of the more vivid expressions of this desire comes from the nineteenth-century poet and essayist Heinrich Heine:

> Mine is a most peaceable disposition. My wishes are: a humble cottage with a thatched roof, but a good bed, good food, the freshest milk and butter, flowers before my window, and a few fine trees before my door; and if God wants to make my happiness complete, he will grant me the joy of seeing some six or seven of my enemies hanging from those trees. Before death I shall, moved in my heart, forgive them all the wrong they did me in their lifetime. One must, it is true, forgive one's enemies—but not before they have been hanged. (cited in Freud 2005: 102)

Perhaps this is amusing because it is grotesque. Let's consider, however, the possibility of an afterlife in which there is some suffering as a result of wickedness, but which is not grotesque or an expression of revenge and resentment. I offer the following in connection with a model of forgiveness, but not the kind of forgiveness described by Heine.

For some, historically and today, part of the problem of evil is that the wicked flourish in this life. When it

comes to addressing wickedness there are several theories of punishment. One is utilitarian: punishment is
justified when it produces some overall good, such as
the ending of oppression or preventing future wickedness by exacting a cost to those who do wrong. This
model might provide some justification for hell to the
extent that if one believes one might end up there due to
one's wickedness then one might have some motivation
for doing good. Many theologians have lamented such
a threatening viewpoint: ideally, one should do good for
goodness' sake, not out of fear of punishment. Another
theory of punishment has to do with correcting the
order of values. When someone has behaved wickedly
they may not have enjoyed it, but they do get their own
way; they did what they did despite the suffering of their
victims. In this case, restoring the order of values would
involve a series of stages involving (ideally) reconciliation. Consider the following model of reconciliation.

When someone harms another and there is to be
reconciliation this would require a dynamic series of
stages involving, for the wrongdoer, confession, repentance, restitution where possible, asking forgiveness, and
reform of character in which the wrongdoer renounces
their wrongful desires and forges a new, more responsible character. Ideally, the person wronged will recognize the sincerity and authenticity of these acts and so
be open (at least in principle) to reconciliation. This is
a complex model which I will fill out a little, though the
main point of raising it here is to make sense of the
possible goodness of the sorrow and suffering involved
in confession and renunciation, and to propose that this
might facilitate a defense of the idea of purgative suffering in life after this life.

In the above scenario sorrow and suffering may enter
at several places, beginning with the confession by the
wrongdoer. A confession made flippantly and without
sorrow is not likely to be credible. The wrongdoer must
renounce any pleasure taken in the wrongdoing. He

must identify himself as the person who did the wrong and then distance himself from the person he was when he did the act. This involves a double movement of identification and renunciation. Ideally, the acts and sorrow should be voluntary. In our own profoundly imperfect world punishment can be an artificial way for society to communicate its values and to induce people to renounce wickedness done and, ideally, to foster beliefs and desires that would inhibit wrongdoing. On this model, the role of punishment is as part of the process of repentance.

The whole process of reconciliation is suffused with controversy. It may be that some acts and persons seem to you to be unforgivable. But in entertaining a defense of a kind of hell after this life, imagine that the sorrow and suffering after death is in some sense purgative. Imagine, for example, that a wrongdoer is made to re-live what he did but from the standpoint of the victim. This would be like the ultimate embodiment of the Golden Rule, in which wrongdoers are brought to understand what they have done to other people, animals, and things by the painful, vivid realization of the cost of his victimizing others. Might this not be a good, bringing about a double-movement in which a person so renounces their past wrongdoing that they (as it were) die to their past self, and come to be regenerated as a new person? This is sometimes described as a model of moral regeneration. If an afterlife were conceived as part of this essential process of death and rebirth, might it then be seen as something that we may wish for out of beneficent love?

A lot would need to be filled in for this model to be robust. What is forgiveness? Can it sometimes be wrong? Must it be freely given or might it ever be morally compelling? Restitution for harms done is sometimes possible in this life, but sometimes not. How might this be worked into the picture? Some readers might object that what I have offered is more of a defense of purgatory than of hell.

I develop some of these issues in the discussion questions at the end of this chapter. But here I will note two factors. First, the above model would fit the traditional idea of purgatory insofar as each person undergoes redemption. But imagine that in such an afterlife whether or not people repent is up to them. In the case of unrepentant creatures the sorrow might then be everlasting. I will not pursue this here; suffice it to note that the model can allow that separation from God might be everlasting, and yet it still be a good that a person is perpetually offered the opportunity of repentance even if it is never taken, just as it may be a good to offer a person a gift even if they never accept it. Second, the model's stress on restitution in a religious context involves resources not available in a secular worldview. In some religions, God has the power to bring everyone back to life. A murderer cannot bring his victim back to life, but an all-powerful, loving God can. It may be part of the process of redemption that a murderer both unite his will with the will of God that the victim not suffer annihilation but be restored to life and fulfillment, and that he seek the forgiveness of the one murdered. All this, of course, will be idle fantasy to those who think an afterlife is impossible. So, let us now turn to consider the bare possibility of life beyond this life.

Is life after this life even possible?

So far in this chapter our treatment of life after death has concerned values. I thought it important to first defend the possible value of life after death before taking up the question of its possibility. After all, if there is no value to life after death, why spend energy debating its possibility?

If you adopt some form of pluralism or dualism, or the view that humans are not solely physical beings, then there is a philosophical opening for an afterlife. For if you are identical with your body and it is annihilated, then it follows that you are annihilated. If you are not so identical, annihilation is not entailed. You may need one other philosophical thesis: namely, that there can be spatial regions not spatially related to this world. Insofar as you believe that personal identity requires some form of embodiment, it may be that any life after this life would need to be considered spatial. Today, some philosophers do think that there can be such different realms, and that not all spatial objects are some distance from, say, the physical reality of this book or the device you are using to read it as an e-book. In fact, a good number of philosophers have recognized various things such as dream images and even our visual field itself as distinct from the mind-independent, physical world around us.

While a materialist view of persons may appear to place belief in an afterlife in jeopardy, this is a thesis that some philosophers have challenged. One option is the possibility of a physical resurrection of persons by God, preserving in being some core element of the body and then recreating, or re-embodying, the person. To the objection that this seems mind-bogglingly complex due to the distribution of matter and energy in the cosmos and the apparent annihilation of bodies, one may reply that a God of limitless power would not be hampered by such appearances and complexity. Other options are available, however; consider two.

Trenton Merricks is a Christian who adopts a materialist view of human persons and yet believes in an individual afterlife. He allows that death involves the ceasing to be of persons, but he thinks we should not rule out the possibility that God can re-create individual persons. This would not have to involve God using the same matter as your body is currently composed of. Here Merricks appeals to what might be called the uniqueness of divine creation. Imagine that God did create you. In doing so, God created *you* instead of some exact replica. And if God created you at some time, can't God recreate you at another? As Merricks writes, to create me the first time,

> God didn't need to make use of matter that had previously been mine, for none had. To do this, God didn't need to secure my continuity, or any kind of continuity at all, with something I had previously been continuous with, because I hadn't previously been. And if God could see to it that I—not just somebody or other—came into existence the first time around, what's to preclude God from doing it again, years after my cremation. (Merricks 2001: 197)

The idea that each individual person has an *essence* has some credibility. Each of us appears to have what philosophers have called a quiddity (a *this-ness*) that is inviolable. If so, perhaps Merricks is correct and we need not worry that the person recreated later would be a mere replica.

The Christian philosopher, Lynne Baker, advocates a constitutional model of personhood. According to Baker, human persons are constituted by their bodies without being identical with them, in the same way that statues are constituted by pieces of marble, copper or bronze, but are not identical with the substances that constitute them (Baker 2000: 91). Baker contends that, because constitution is not identity, one can maintain both that persons are currently composed of an exclusively physical body, and that they may survive the perishing of this body. Her position may seem puzzling at first, but in a common sense context we can readily distinguish between constitution and identity. The marble making up Michelangelo's statue *David* can be seen as a distinct object, for one could destroy the statue but still have the marble. You could reconstruct the marble in the form of Mickey Mouse and Michelangelo's masterpiece would be replaced by a Walt Disney character. Arguably, you might also slowly replace

David bit by bit until all the original marble was gone and yet the statue remained. These types of alterations suggest to Baker that a person might survive the destruction of her body.

> The constitution view can offer those who believe in immaterial souls ... almost everything that they want— without the burden of making sense of how there can be immaterial souls in the natural world. For example, human persons can survive change of body; truths about persons are not exhausted by truths about bodies; persons have causal powers that their bodies would not have if they did not constitute persons; there is a fact of the matter about which, if any, future person is I ... The constitution view allows that a person's resurrection body may be nonidentical with her earthly body. According to the constitution view, it is logically possible that a person have different bodies at different times; whether anyone ever changes bodies or not, the logical possibility is built into the constitution view. (Baker 2005: 387)

There are yet more materialist options, but perhaps these two are enough to provide some reason why even a materialist should not rule out the possibility of life after death. (For a recent, cogent defense of the possibility of life after death see Eddebo 2017.)

Revelation, miracles, prayers

Not all religions involve claims about revelation. Buddhism, Confucianism, and Daoism do not claim to be based upon or supported by divine revelation. Matters are different in the Abrahamic faiths and in some forms of Hinduism. Let us briefly consider a philosophy of revelation, miracles, and prayers.

If the divine is believed to be good and purposive or, going further, a lover of creation, then it seems one should be open to the possibility that this divine reality would be revealed or disclosed in human history, and perhaps even today. This is depicted in various sacred scriptures in different traditions. The revelation may take the form of divine commands (more on this in the final section of this chapter), or of the expression of divine love and providential care, an occasion for prayer, repentance, forgiveness, thanksgiving, and reconciliation with God and people. Revelation has also been appealed to in the establishment of rites, such as worship or the hallowing of relationships and rites of passage (the seeking of divine blessing on children, covenants, marriage, dying and the burial of the dead).

Why believe in any divine revelation? One basis would be the kind of inferences discussed in the argument from religious experience in Chapter 4. But another possible source of evidence may come from reported miracles. The best-known critic of the case for revelation based on reported miracles is David Hume. Hume's chief objection rests on a concept of intellectual responsibility:

> A wise man, therefore, proportions his belief to the evidence. In such conclusions as are founded on an infallible experience, he expects the event with the last degree of assurance, and regards his past experience as a full *proof* of the future existence of that event. In other cases, he proceeds with more caution: He weighs the opposite experiments: He considers which side is supported by the greater number of experiments: to that side he inclines, with doubt and hesitation; and when at last he has fixed his judgment, the evidence exceeds not what we properly call *probability*. All probability, then, supposes an opposition of experiments and observations, where one side is found to overbalance the other, and to produce a degree of evidence, proportioned to the superiority. A hundred instances or experiments on one side, and fifty on another, afford a doubtful expectation of any event; though a hundred uniform experiments, with only one that is contradictory,

reasonably begets a pretty strong degree of assurance. In all cases, we must balance the opposite experiments, where they are opposite, and deduct the *smaller number* from the greater, in order to know the exact force of the superior evidence. (Hume 1902: section X, part 1)

Hume therefore concludes that "the proof against a miracle ... is as entire as any arguments from experience can possibly be imagined." His objection has been further defended by Antony Flew, J. L. Mackie, and others.

The most widespread theistic response to this objection has been to question whether Hume has simply begged the question. If one assumes at the outset that there have never been exceptions to the laws of nature, then one has assumed from the beginning that there have never been any miracles. It is not clear, however, whether Hume does beg the question in this fashion. Arguably, the strength of his position is that he highlights the great weight of testimony on behalf of the laws of nature and the significantly more slender testimony on behalf of exceptions to these laws. J. L. Mackie articulates this Humean strategy as follows:

It is ... not enough for the defender of a miracle to cast doubt (as well he might) on the certainty of our knowledge of the law of nature that seems to have been violated. For he must himself say that this *is* a law of nature: otherwise the reported event will not be miraculous. That is, he must in effect *concede* to Hume that the antecedent improbability of this event is as high as it could be, hence that, apart from the testimony, we have the strongest possible grounds for believing that the alleged event did not occur. This event must, by the miracle advocate's own admission, be contrary to a genuine, not merely a supposed law of nature, and therefore maximally improbable. It is this maximal improbability that the weight of the testimony would have to overcome. (Mackie 1982: 25)

If Mackie is right, an argument for theism based on the appeal to miracles will always be at a disadvantage.

A second theistic reply is to challenge the use of probability employed by Mackie and other Humeans. Stephen Evans points out how Humean arguments presuppose a substantial background of philosophical commitments:

> The defender of miracles may claim that whether miracles occur depends largely on whether God exists, what kind of God he is, and what purposes he has. Given enough knowledge of God and his purposes in relation to human history, occurrence of a miracle might be in some situations highly probable, or at least not nearly so improbable as Hume suggests ... In the absence of any firm knowledge about God and his purposes, it would still be rash to claim with Hume that the probability of a miracle is vanishingly small. Rather it would appear more reasonable to conclude that it is hard, if not impossible, to estimate the a priori probability of a miracle; and therefore one should try to look at the evidence for miracles with a somewhat open, though cautiously skeptical, mind. (Evans 1985: 113)

Alvin Plantinga similarly notes that Mackie seems to presuppose that God does not regularly interact with the cosmos:

> Why should we suppose that a violation of a law of nature (taken Mackie's way) is maximally improbable (prior to testimony) on our evidence? On Mackie's conception, a law of nature describes the way the world works when it is not interfered with (for example, by God); but why should we think it is particularly improbable that it be interfered with? The antecedent probability of a miracle, for me, depends upon what I know and believe about the world; but perhaps I have no reason to suppose that the world is not regularly interfered with. Why couldn't interferences with nature be the rule rather than the exception? Perhaps God

doesn't ordinarily leave nature to herself, but takes a
hand in what happens. (Plantinga 1986: 112)

I leave the case for and against belief in miracles in the
reader's hands. The term "miracle" comes from the
Latin *miraculum*, for *object of wonder*, and it may be
that what religious believers principally respond to in
the miraculous is more a matter of wondrous events
rather than a violation of the laws of nature. Since I
began this treatment recording Hume's famous case
against miracles, I will end by citing Grace Jantzen's
brazen claim that any extraordinary evidence for some
miracle would not necessarily bring us to revise our
concept of the laws of nature:

> If a situation arose in which there were compelling
> evidence for believing that Jesus rose from the dead, a
> revision of our supposed natural laws would hardly be
> the appropriate response ... Where there is a single
> exception to a perfectly well established and well
> understood law, and one that is inexplicable unless one
> appeals to divine intervention (in which case it assumes
> enormous significance), what can be gained by making
> the nomological read, "All men are mortal except those
> who have an unknown quality, observed on only one
> occasion and hitherto accountable for only by divine
> intervention." ... The skeptical response would be
> inadequate. (Jantzen 1979: 325)

One important dimension of some revelation texts is
that of prayer. There are many forms of prayer: praise,
confession, laments, petitions, placations, and so on. In
the chapter on divine attributes, we briefly considered
worship. For those theists who highlight God as essentially good, worship is more like having a feeling of awe
in the presence of divine goodness than praising a
powerful ego. Some philosophers are vexed by the idea
that petitionary prayers are fitting in relation to the God
of theism. Consider the following: If God is omniscient

then there is no need for us to inform God of our desires and needs. If God is perfectly good, then God will do what is perfectly good whether we petition God to do good or not. There is therefore no good involved in petitioning God to do good.

Several replies to this are possible. First, the confession of a wrongdoing may itself be good even if the person you are confessing to already knows you did the wrong. The confession might be part of the process of redemption discussed above. Publicly confessing to an omniscient God can be a way to inform others in one's community of one's wrongdoing and provide a context for repentance. Second, insofar as God gives us freedom, and some of the goods in this world depend upon our responsible use of that freedom, why would God not allow some goods to be realized by God as a result of free petition? Consider a short thought experiment. Imagine you are considering adopting a child and that doing so would be good for both you and the child. You do so, without responding to any petition. Now, imagine the same state of affairs but this time your adoption of the child is motivated (in part) by petitions—from the child, from the biological parents, from your spouse.... Arguably, the latter case involves a good that the first does not. Both are good (by hypothesis), but the second case includes the additional good of others participating in the good act. So, I suggest the case against petitionary prayer is not obvious.

Religious and secular values

Some religious values seem to corroborate secular values. Consider, for example, the widespread use of the Golden Rule (the list is taken from Meister 2012):

> Confucianism: "Never do to others what you would not like them to do to you."—The Analects of Confucius 15.23

Hinduism: "One should not behave towards others in a way which is disagreeable to oneself. This is the essence of morality. All other activities are due to selfish desire."—The Hindu Mahabharata, Anushasan Parva XIII 113.8

Buddhism: "He who for the sake of happiness hurts others, who also wants happiness, shall not hereafter find happiness. He who for the sake of happiness does not hurt others, who also want happiness, shall hereafter find happiness."—The Dhammapada 131

Judaism: "What is hateful to you, do not do to your neighbor: that is the whole Torah; all the rest of it is commentary; go and learn."—Talmud, Shabbat 31a

Christianity: "Do to others as you would have them do to you."—Luke 6:31.

Islam: "No man is a true believer unless he desires for his brother that which he desires for himself."—Muhammad, from the Hadith, Muslim imam, 71–2

Religious values have a variety of relations to secular values: they can reinforce or magnify them, or be in opposition to them, and they can set up independent values that seem neutral with respect to the secular point of view.

In terms of reinforcement or intensification, some religious claims endorse what many secularists think: we should care about the environment, including the welfare of non-human animals; we should assist those in need, especially the innocent who are subject to undeserved harms; we should not murder; we should keep our promises, and so on. Religious values sometimes conflict with secular values, however, insofar as they call for the fostering of higher values or different values. Some religions, for example, are less friendly to free-market solutions to economic and social problems than some secularists, preferring an ethic that provides greater aid to the vulnerable. Some religions are anti-capital punishment and advance particular conceptions of family, sexuality, wealth, and drug and alcohol use different to those of some secularists. Philosophers have addressed many of these and other issues. Given limitations on space, we will here consider only three vexing philosophical matters: religious commands to do what seems wrong; religious medical ethics in relation to physician-assisted suicide; and the role of religious values in a pluralistic democracy.

One of the troubling events in the Book of Genesis is the apparent command of God for Abraham to sacrifice his son Isaac. Abraham binds Isaac and is ready to kill him as an offering when an angel intervenes to stop the sacrifice. A goat is offered as a substitute. Probably the clearest philosophical response to this narrative is by Immanuel Kant who maintained that child sacrifice is clearly wrong, an all-just God would not command this, and therefore Abraham should have disbelieved an ostensible divine revelation that God would command something clearly unjust. A related response is that the meaning behind the story is that child sacrifice is wrong; whether God made the command or not, the point is that such a sacrifice should not be made. This is a bit more troubling than Kant's position insofar as this second approach allows that God may command something that is wrong, even if this is part of God revealing to persons that what is commanded is wrong. Another philosophical approach is to claim that God is the author of all life and if God did indeed command a child sacrifice, that would have been morally permissible. It has been argued that just as God cannot commit robbery by taking some property of yours (for as Creator all things belong to God), God cannot commit murder (unjustly killing a person) for all creatures belong to God. Yet another, slightly different view is that religious duties (such as following divine commands) can supersede or suspend that which is ethical. I leave this matter for you to reflect on.

In relation to medical ethics, there are various areas where religious beliefs and values come into play. There are some religious traditions according to which all life is sacred, and thus abortion involves the violation of the sanctity of life. Some traditions hold that blood transfusions, stem cell research, the use of animals in scientific experiments in which the animals suffer or are killed, the sale of human organs, are wrong. Here let us consider why some religious ethics prohibit suicide, including physician-assisted suicide as an example of tension between secular and religious values.

In some mainstream secular ethical traditions, great stress is placed on autonomy, the rightful exercise of freedom by (sane, fully informed) individuals to make their own choices about whether to live or die. Currently, this is often debated about cases of when an individual has an incurable, painful illness. Some religious traditions allow for some actions in which physicians may administer a drug (typically morphine) that is primarily intended to reduce (or eliminate) suffering but has the foreseen consequence of ending the life of the patient. It is argued that this is not a case of mercy killing, but of relieving unbearable suffering. But why would any religion prohibit a person taking his own life under dire circumstances or taking the morphine with the intent of ending the life of a patient? One reason is that it is believed that all life belongs to God and that by taking one's own life (or someone else doing so, with or without one's consent) involves a kind of "playing God." On this view, there is an important value in a "natural death," one that occurs without any agent's deliberate killing or allowing persons to die when this is preventable.

Debate over this issue in terms of religious and secular ethics often focuses on defending or challenging the rightness or coherence of a person "playing God." For those defending physician-assisted suicide (or suicide in general), the notion of "playing God" rests on a mistaken view of God's providence. It is argued that we should not believe that God so providentially controls the world that the death of persons only occurs when unassisted by human causes. After all, human intervention occurs routinely in medical practice; just as we do not think that taking aspirin is "playing God" in some offensive fashion, it is argued that we should not think we are usurping God's role in administering morphine. I leave the debate in your hands.

As a third example of the interplay of the religious and the secular, consider how religious values might come into play in a pluralistic democratic republic. Let's take as our example the teaching in many, but not all, religions that capital punishment is wrong. Imagine that if we do not invoke religious values, there is a powerful case for capital punishment. Imagine that there is good evidence that capital punishment can be administered fairly (without bias in terms of race, gender or the economic standing of the accused) and that it actually does more effectively make future crime less likely. (For the record, I do not believe this to be the case, but I am proposing this as a possibility.) Imagine that you have religious reasons (perhaps based on Buddhist views of compassion or you are a Roman Catholic), would it be fitting for you to vote against capital punishment on religious grounds when not everyone in your society adopts your religion?

As you may expect by now, philosophers have taken different positions. Some philosophers who (as it happens) are religious practitioners themselves, have taken the view that it is wrong to vote or legislate on any grounds other than secular ones. On their view, it is vital that religious persons not impose their values on a general public that includes "non-believers." Others have taken the view that to separate one's religious views from one's views about what is good politically and socially is to court a kind of schizophrenia and a privatization of religion. It is asking too much of each other to bracket our most central values when we vote or act in the public square.

This survey of only three areas of tension is only scratching the surface, but I hope it stimulates further thought rather than only serving as a report on current debates. These topics are alive and, as I seek to offer in the final chapter, there are ways you may engage in these and other topics in multiple ways.

Discussion questions

In this chapter, some fantastic literature has been used in relation to questions about long life. You may find it philosophically interesting to engage with classic and contemporary portraits of life after death, from the work of Homer to Dante's *Divine Comedy* to Charles Williams' extraordinary *Descent into Hell*. The latter offers a compelling story of a person's damnation. For someone finding redemption in life after death, see Williams' *Ash Wednesday*. In your view, in what ways can fictional narratives contribute to the exploration of possibilities in philosophy of religion?

In his book, *Death and Eternal Life*, John Hick (1976) offers a blended portrait of life after death in which he draws on multiple religious traditions to offer an inclusive, sweeping model of what life after death might be like. Hick defends a form of universalism, according to which all persons will be redeemed. Is the plausibility of belief in an afterlife increased if the apparent conflicting accounts of an afterlife, historically and today, may be seen as compatible and even mutually enriching?

The classic understanding of forgiveness is that one person forgives another when she renounces (or at least moderates) her resentment of another person because of some perceived wrong. This may fit many but not all cases of forgiveness, as some people may be able to forgive others and yet be incapable of resentment (so there would be no resentment to renounce or moderate), I have defended an alternative according to which a person forgives another when she ceases to blame them for a (perceived) wrong. What is your view? Here are some of the questions that a robust account of forgiveness needs to address: Can forgiveness ever be a duty? Is it possible (or good) to forgive a person who has not asked for forgiveness? Can forgiveness involve a process that takes time? If you have truly forgiven someone, can this be rescinded? Is it possible to forgive someone for a wrong and yet insist on them being punished for the wrong? Can one truly forgive another person and yet not seek any reconciliation with them?

In some religious traditions, there is an obligation to love others as well as oneself. Do you believe that love is something that is under a person's voluntary control? If it is not under our control, how might we be under an obligation to love?

For a survey of multiple diverse secular and religious arguments and values, see the Ethics website authored by faculty and students at St. Olaf College: https://pages.stolaf.edu/ein

7

Getting Involved in Philosophy of Religion Today

In the introduction, I noted how I found the practice of philosophy of religion, and in particular philosophy of religion, a liberation and a refuge from the hostile disrespectful exchanges I found in the culture I grew up in. As I write, the culture in the west, the United States specifically, seems just as divisive as when I was a youth. I hope that you might find the practice of philosophy today enriching and a refreshing alternative to entrenched quarreling. What follows are some suggestions about how to enter the world(s) of philosophy of religion as a practitioner, and not just a reader or spectator.

One great way to practice philosophy of religion and to foster friendship is to create reading groups. Even if you are currently a student, undergraduate or graduate, it can be rewarding to be part of a reading group in which there is mutual support and ongoing events in which to practice philosophy without grades. Reading books and attending lectures (whether in life or by way of viewing or hearing lectures in philosophy of religion offered by, for example, the Great Courses company) can be great, but like learning a language, it is often best done in practice when one can make mistakes and be open to friendly suggestions for improvement.

If you are not enrolled in a college or university, but can access one, I suggest you research when lectures are offered in philosophy of religion and are open to the public. If you are not a member of a college or a university, the term used to describe a person who is undertaking scholarship is an "independent scholar." So in emails or other modes of introducing yourself to professors, chairs of departments, and so on, is to introduce yourself as an independent scholar living in the area and interested in attending any philosophy lectures/events open to the public. Many of the great, early modern philosophers in Europe such as Descartes, Anne Conway, Locke, Margaret Cavendish, Leibniz, Spinoza, Berkeley, Hume, J.S. Mill, were not attached to universities as professors.

Some universities and colleges have institutes that specialize in philosophy of religion, and these may sponsor events you can attend either for free or for a nominal fee. Probably one of the best known in the English-speaking world is the Center for Philosophy of Religion at the University of Notre Dame in Indiana. The Center has a website which is full of great references to introductions to philosophy of religion, a calendar of events, and more. Other important centers for philosophy of religion are the Rutgers Center for philosophy of Religion at Rutgers University, the Centre for Philosophy of Religion at the University of Roehampton (formerly at Heythrop College), the Centre for Philosophy and Religion at the University of Glasgow, the Centre of Theology and Philosophy at the University of Nottingham, the Institute for Philosophy and Religion at Boston University, and The John Hick Center for Philosophy of Religion at the University of Birmingham. If you are drawn to particular figures in the history of philosophy, there are sometimes centers dedicated to them you can visit and engage the scholars working there. At St. Olaf College, we have the Kierkegaard Library which welcomes scholars from around the world who wish to study, write on and discuss the work of the nineteenth century Danish philosopher Søren Kierkegaard. The Library hosts an international conference every two years with over a hundred scholars. The Library also has scholarships you may apply for to do a residency at the Library.

Doing searches on the Internet for conferences in philosophy of religion can yield great results for opportunities to meet some of the leading persons contributing to the field today. See the websites for the British Society for Philosophy of Religion, the European Society for the Philosophy of Religion, the International Philosophy of Religion Association, the American Philosophical Association and the American Academy of Religion to get started. Depending on your philosophical or religious orientation there are a host of societies that will be of interest. So, for those who are Christians with philosophical interests, you might do searches for: the American Catholic Philosophical Association, the Canadian Society of Christian Philosophers, the Evangelical Philosophical Society, the Society of Christian Philosophers. Some of these societies host debates, as one can find on The Secular Web which hosted the debate God or Blind Nature? Overseen by Paul Draper, a leading philosopher of religion today. There are also undergraduate philosophy conferences in virtually all the states in the USA that can be sites for philosophy of religion.

At philosophy conferences it is quite common for presentations to take around 45 to 60 minutes and then it is often the case that there is a commentator who has been appointed to respond to the lecture/presentation. In the introduction, I commended the Golden Rule (treat other philosophies as you would like your own to be treated) and being a Good Samaritan (assisting other philosophers in difficulty). Bear in mind that I present these as ideal practices among lovers of wisdom (the literal meaning of philosophy), but it is not the case that *every official professional philosopher practices these.* Please do not be shocked when (sadly) some few philosophers at conferences (and sometimes in print) are hostile and competitive, and see themselves more as fearless warriors than calm, open minded, compassionate sages. I have been to jubilant conferences that have been life-changing (in a good way!) and also witnessed exchanges between philosophers that have been (for lack of a better word) unfortunate. Still, I can report that there is a huge amount of more grace, care, and (good) passionate commitments to respectful inquiry than the opposite! One might also take heart that the very first philosophers of religion who wrote in English (the Cambridge Platonists in the seventeenth century) saw love as their central theme, love between persons, love of nature and of the divine. Their stress on love earned them credit for helping lay the groundwork culturally for the movement to end slavery (as argued in *The Problem of Slavery in Western Culture* by David B. Davis). For an impressive portrait of a loving philosophical community, see the following account of the great companionship that Augustine wrote about in his *Confessions* (IV, 8):

> There were joys to be found in their company which still more captivated my mind—the charms of talking and laughing together and kindly giving way to each other's wishes, reading elegantly written books together, sharing jokes and delighting to honour one another, disagreeing occasionally but without rancour, as a person might disagree with themselves, and lending piquancy by that rare disagreement to our much more frequent accord. We would teach and learn from each other, sadly missing any who were absent and blithely welcoming them when they returned. Such signs of friendship sprang from the hearts of friends who loved and knew their love returned, signs to be read in smiles,

words, glances and a thousand gracious gestures. So were sparks kindled and our minds were fused inseparably, out of many becoming one.

The best online resource for philosophy in general and the philosophy of religion in particular is the free online Stanford Encyclopedia of Philosophy. Some interactive sites, such as Ask Philosophers, offer an opportunity of asking questions of leading philosophers from around the world. Many nations have active philosophical societies. See, for example, the website of the Iranian Philosophical Society (IPS).

In terms of books, many of the leading presses in the English-speaking world have books in philosophy of religion. For great proposals about leading books consult the Stanford Encyclopedia of Philosophy or the different philosophy of religion companions and handbooks published by Oxford, Cambridge, Wiley-Blackwell, Routledge, Bloomsbury, the University of Notre Dame Press. Some presses specialize in particular religious or secular positions. For example, Prometheus Press publishes many books critical of theism and organized religion, while Eerdmans or Baker publish works supportive of a Christian worldview.

In terms of journals in philosophy of religion, here are some for you to consider (the list is selective): Ars Disputandi, Contemporary Buddhism: An Interdisciplinary Journal, European Journal for Philosophy of Religion, Faith and Philosophy, Journal of Buddhist Ethics, Journal of Indian Philosophy and Religion, The Journal of Religion, Journal of Religious Ethics, Journal of Theological Studies, International Journal for Philosophy of Religion, Modern Theology, Open Theology, Philo, Philosophia Christi, Religious Studies, Sophia, the Toronto Journal of Theology. Most mainline journals in philosophy include philosophy of religion, for example: American Philosophical Quarterly, Analysis, Ethics, Mind, Philosophical Quarterly, Philosophy (published by the Royal Society of Philosophy), Philosophy and Phenomenological Research, and more. You can find information on submitting papers to these journals online. Many, but not all of them, review submissions blind (that is, the reviewers do not know the name of the authors). Reviews of submissions can take anywhere from a few weeks to three months.

If you are considering going on in philosophy of religion at the graduate level, you may consider Ph.D. programs at the following institutions (among many others): Baylor University, Boston College, Boston University, Cambridge University, University of Notre Dame, Oxford University, Loyola University, Oslo University, Purdue University, Princeton University, University of Glasgow, Rutgers University, St. Louis University, Uppsala University (Sweden), the University of Toronto, Vanderbilt University, Yale University. The list is partial, but a good beginning. Philosophy of religion may also be found at leading theological institutions such as Harvard Divinity School, Yale Divinity School, Princeton Theological Seminary, and elsewhere. You would need a Ph.D. to be a good candidate for a teaching position at a college or university, but a Masters is often sufficient for teaching at community colleges. Masters degrees in philosophy are available at a number of schools, including Tufts University and the University of Rhode Island. If you are seeking a Ph.D., it is common for you to receive a Masters in the process.

You can find opportunities to do philosophy of religion not just in academic settings or private parties and reading groups; it may also be found in the philosophy of popular culture books published by Blackwell and Open Court. I have contributed with some philosophy of religion in books on the Hobbit, Harry Potter, Star Wars, and Narnia (among others).

Wherever you are in the world, there will be some philosophy of religion being practiced at least in the major metropolitan areas that support higher education. I have found this to be true in my travels doing philosophy in Latin America, Europe, the Middle East, Russia, China, and elsewhere. Among all the international meetings of philosophers, the most well established is the World Congress of Philosophy, which has been held every five years since 1900. Philosophy of religion has been a part of each meeting. The first meeting was in Paris, while the 2018 meeting was in Beijing, China.

Please feel free to contact me personally if I can be of help to you in exploring philosophy of religion, as part of the overall undertaking of the love of wisdom.

References

Abraham, W., and Aquino, F. (eds) (2017) *The Oxford Handbook of the Epistemology of Theology*, Oxford: Oxford University Press.

Anderson, P. (2014) "Why Feminist Philosophy of Religion? An Interview with Pamela Sue Anderson," *Logoi: A Publication of the Center for Philosophy of Religion at Notre Dame*, 1:11–13.

Baker, L. (2000) *Persons and Bodies*, Cambridge: Cambridge University Press.

Baker, L. (2005) "Death and the Afterlife," in W. Wainwright (ed.), *The Oxford Handbook of Philosophy of Religion*, Oxford: Oxford University Press.

Boethius (1897) *Consolations of Philosophy*, trans. H. James, London: Dent.

Cain, C. (2015) "Cosmic Origins and Genesis: A Religious Response," in C. Clifford (ed.), *Re-Vision: A New Look at the Relationship Between Science and Religion*, Lanham: University Press of America.

Camus, A. (1961) "The Unbeliever and Christians," in *Resistance, Rebellion and Death*, New York: Knopf.

Chesterton, G. (2006) *Orthodoxy*, Peabody: Hendrickson Publishers.

Chomsky, N. (1980) *Rules and Representations*, New York: Columbia University Press.

Clark, K. (2017) "Imaginings," *European Journal for Philosophy of Religion*, 9:1.

Cohn-Sherbok, D. (1990) "Jewish Faith and the Holocaust," *Religious Studies*, 26:2.

Dawkins, R. (2006) *The God Delusion*, New York: Bantam Books.

Dennett, D. (1991) *Consciousness Explained*, Boston: Little, Brown.

Eddebo, J. (2017) *Death and the Self: A Metaphysical Investigation of the Rationality of Afterlife Belief in the Contemporary Intellectual Climate*, Uppsala: Uppsala University Press.

Ellis, F. (2014) *God, Value, and Nature*, Oxford: Oxford University Press.

Evans, S. (1985) *Philosophy of Religion*, Downers Grove: Intervarsity.

Freud, S. (2005) *Civilization and Its Discontents*, New York: W.W. Norton.

Gutting, G. (2015) *What Philosophers Can Do*, New York: W.W. Norton.

Hick, J. (1976) *Death and Eternal Life*, San Francisco: Harper and Row.

—— (1989) *An Interpretation of Religion: Human Responses to the Transcendent*, New Haven: Yale University Press.

Hobbes, T. (1998) *Leviathan*, ed. J. Gaskin, Oxford: Oxford University Press.

Honderich, T. (ed.) (1995) *The Oxford Companion to Philosophy*, Oxford: Oxford University Press.

Hospers, J. (1997) *An Introduction to Philosophical Analysis*, London: Routledge.

Hume, D. (1902) *Enquiry Concerning Human Understanding*, ed. D. Selby-Bigge, *Hume Enquiries*, Oxford: Oxford University Press.

James, W. (2000) *Pragmatism and Other Writings*, ed. G. Gunn, New York: Penguin.

Jantzen, G. (1979) "Hume on Miracles, History and Politics," *Christian Scholars Review*, 8.

Kitcher, P. (2014) *Life after Faith*, New Haven: Yale University Press.

Kwan, K-M. (2011) *The Rainbow of Experiences, Critical Trust, and God: A Defense of Holistic Empiricism*, London: Continuum.

Lamont, J. (2004) *Divine Faith*, London: Routledge.

Lockwood, M. (2003) "Consciousness and the Quantum Worlds," in Q. Smith (ed.), *Consciousness: New Philosophical Perspectives*, Oxford: Clarendon.

Lund, D. (2005) *The Conscious Self: The Immaterial Center of Subjective States*, Amherst: Humanity Books.

McFague, S. (2008) *A New Climate for Theology*, Minneapolis: Fortress Press.

McGinn, C. (1991) *The Problem of Consciousness*, Hoboken: Wiley-Blackwell.

Mackie, J. L. (1982) *The Miracle of Theism*, Oxford: Clarendon Press.

Martin, M. (1990) *Atheism*, Philadelphia: Temple University Press.

Mautner, T. (ed.) (1996) *A Dictionary of Philosophy*, Oxford: Wiley-Blackwell.

Meister, C. (2012) *Evil: A Guide for the Perplexed*, London: A&C Black.

Merricks, T. (2001) *How to Live Forever Without Saving Your Soul: Physicalism and Immortality*, in K. Corcoran (ed.), *Soul, Body, and Survival*, Ithaca: Cornell University Press.

Nagawawa, Y. (2017) *Maximal God: A New Defence of Perfect Being Theism*, Oxford: Oxford University Press.

O'Connor, T. (2008) *Theism and Ultimate Explanation: The Necessary Shape of Contingency*, Hoboken: Wiley-Blackwell.

Papineau, D. and Dennett, D. (2017) "Papineau vs Dennett: A Philosophical Dispute," *Times Literary Supplement*, August 2, https://www.the-tls.co.uk/articles/public/dennett-papineau-debate.

Pinker, S. (2013) "Science Is Not Your Enemy," *New Republic*, August 7, https://newrepublic.com/article/114127/science-not-enemy-humanities.

Plantinga, A. (1986) "Is Theism Really a Miracle?," *Faith and Philosophy*, 3:2.

Pruss, A. and Rasmussen, J. (2018) *Necessary Existence*, Oxford: Oxford University Press.

Rachels, J. (1996) *Can Ethics Provide Answers?*, Blue Ridge: Rowman and Littlefield.

Rolston, H. (2003) "Does Nature need to be Redeemed?," in C. Taliaferro and P. Griffiths (eds), *Philosophy of Religion: A Reader*, Oxford: Blackwell Press.

Ruse, M. (2014) "Atheism and Science," in S. Fuller, M. Stenmark and U. Sackartason (eds), *The Customization of Science*, New York: Palgrave.

Russell, Be. (1927) *An Outline of Philosophy*, London: Routledge.

Russell, Br. (2009) *Review of The Elusive God: Reorienting Religious Epistemology*, by P. Moser, *Notre Dame Philosophical Reviews*, https://ndpr.nd.edu/news/the-elusive-god-reorienting-religious-epistemology.

National Academy of Sciences and Institute of Medicine (2008) "Compatibility of Science and Religion," http://www.nas.edu/evolution/Compatibility.html.

Shankara (1970) *Shankara's Crest-Jewel of Discrimination*, trans. Swami Prabhavanda and C. Isherwood, New York: Mentor Books.

St. Augustine of Hippo (1997) *Confessions*, in *The Works of Saint Augustine*, trans. The Augustinian Heritage Institute, New York: New City Press.

Stenmark, M. (2004) *How to Relate Religion and Science: A Multidimensional Model*, Grand Rapids: Eerdmans.

Swinburne, R. (1991) *The Existence of God*, Oxford: Clarendon.

Trigg, R. (2015) *Beyond Matter*, Conshohocken: Templeton Foundation Press.

The World Council of Religious Leaders (2002) "About the World Council," http://www.millenniumpeacesummit.org/wc_about.html.

UNESCO (2017) "Philosophy Day at UNESCO," http://www.unesco.org/new/en/social-and-human-sciences/themes/most-programme/humanities-and-philosophy/philosophy-day-at-unesco.

Ward, K. (2007) *Is Religion Dangerous?* Grand Rapids: Eerdmans.

—— (2008) *The Big Questions in Science and Religion*, Conshohocken: Templeton Foundation Press.

Wettstein, H. (2012) *The Significance of Religious Experience*, Oxford: Oxford University Press.

Yandell, K. (1984) *Christianity and Philosophy*, Grand Rapids: William Eerdmans.

Zagzebski, L. (2001) "Recovering Understanding," in Mattias Steup (ed.), *Knowledge, Truth, and Duty*, Oxford: Oxford University Press.